# Network Science, A Decade Later

## The Internet and Classroom Learning

# Network Science, A Decade Later

## The Internet and Classroom Learning

Alan Feldman

Cliff Konold

& Bob Coulter

with Brian Conroy

Charles Hutchison

& Nancy London

Foreword by

Barbara Means

This project was undertaken by TERC, Inc.,
Cambridge, Massachusetts. Funded in part by a
grant from the National Science Foundation.

TERC

**IEA** **Lawrence Erlbaum Associates, Publishers**

2000  Mahwah, New Jersey          London

Cover: Map reprinted with permission of Journey North.
www.learner.org/jnorth
The map represents Monarch butterfly migrations and shows the week in the spring of
1999 that students reported seeing the first Monarch butterfly in their area.

The final camera copy for this work was prepared by the author, and therefore the
publisher takes no responsibility for consistency or correctness of typographical style.

 This project was undertaken by TERC, Inc., Cambridge, Massachusetts. Funded
in part by a grant from the National Science Foundation.

TERC

This material is based upon work supported by the National Science Foundation under
Grant Nos. RED-9454704, RED-9155743, and REC-9725228. Any opinions, findings,
and conclusions or recommendations expressed in this material are those of the authors
and do not necessarily reflect views of the National Science Foundation.

Lawrence Erlbaum Associates, Inc., Publishers
10 Industrial Avenue
Mahwah, New Jersey 07430

Cover design by Kathryn Houghtaling Lacey

**Library of Congress Cataloging-in-Publication Data**

Network science, a decade later: the internet and classroom learning
    Alan Feldman...(et al.).
        p. cm.
    Includes bibliographical references and index
    ISBN 0-8058-3425-7 (alk. paper).--ISBN 0-8058-3426-5 (pbk. : alk. paper)
    1. Science--United States--Computer-assisted instruction. 2. Internet (Computer
    network) in education--United States. I. Title. II. Title: Network science.
    LB1583.3.F44 2000                                                      99-38653
    507.8'5--dc21                                                          CIP

Books published by Lawrence Erlbaum Associates are printed on acid-free paper, and
their bindings are chosen for strength and durability.

Printed in the United States of America
10  9  8  7  6  5  4  3  2  1

*In memory of*

*Mildred Shapiro (Midge)*
*teacher • mentor • friend*

# Contents

# Foreword

O ver the last decade, a tremendous investment has been made in Internet access for schools. In 1990, few U.S. schools had Internet connections, and many of these were low-speed, dial-up modem connections from a single computer. By 1994, the proportion of schools with Internet access was significant—at 35%—and by 1997, it had risen sharply to 75%.

School connections are just a rough indicator of access, of course, because they may be in an administrator's office that is off limits or in a lab or media center that is shared by so many classes that teachers cannot count on access when they need it. Thus, the figures for classroom Internet access are more pertinent, and here the change has been just as dramatic. In 1994, the proportion of U.S. classrooms with Internet access was just 3%; by 1997, it had grown to 27%. In early 1999, the U.S. Department of Education announced that over half the classrooms in the United States have Internet access; by the fall of 1999, the Department expects 80% of U.S. classrooms to be online. President Clinton's 1996 call for getting every classroom in America on the Internet no longer sounds like far-fetched political rhetoric. With so much progress on the infrastructure front, educators today are confronting the question, "Now what?"

Certainly, supporters of this multibillion-dollar investment have believed that network access would contribute significantly to the improvement of education. One of the best-articulated applications of Internet access with promise for substantive contributions to learning is network science. Rather than simply searching for information and copying text or graphics, students in network science projects perform activities essential to the practice of science—taking measurements according to structured protocols, both contributing to and drawing from scientific databases, analyzing and interpreting data, and communicating and discussing their conclusions. The vision of students, teachers, and classrooms collaborating on investigations and sharing data and insights through the global network, in fact, preceded the World Wide Web. Without any of the ease of use associated with the graphical layout and interactive features of modern web sites, the National Geographic Kids Network project nevertheless pioneered classrooms sharing data with each other in 1989.

Yet a decade later, despite the greater usability of today's web interfaces, the best efforts of a large number of talented people, the vast improvement in computer and Internet access, and the conceptual compatibility of network science programs with national science and mathematics standards, collaborations between classrooms and distant partners over the network remain the exception rather than the rule. Becker and Anderson's national survey of teachers in 1998, for example, found that only 6% had their students collaborate with other classrooms over the Internet during the 1997–1998 school year.

Why are network science programs so slow to take hold? When they do get started, why are so few teachers taking advantage of the opportunity to have their students collaborate with distant classrooms? Feldman, Konold, and Coulter address these questions based on over a decade of experience with a succession of network-based science programs. Much of the pioneering work in cross-classroom science inquiry was done at TERC. The candid reflections of these authors help us understand the classroom realities that often undermine the ideal of student scientists working on significant investigations through the Net.

Two aspects of their analysis strike me as fundamental. First, the teacher's role is pivotal in inquiry-oriented science teaching, regardless of whether telecommunications are involved. Oversimplified characterizations of the teacher's role as that of "guide on the side," responding to student requests for assistance, can leave the erroneous impression that students can be launched into an investigation posed by a curriculum developer with little teacher involvement beyond availability for responding to questions. Detailed studies of classroom interaction suggest that, on the contrary, successful student investigations occur in classrooms where teachers give students considerable responsibility but still actively shape the nature of both their queries and their analyses and interpretations.

Technology proponents have suggested that we need to transform teachers into proficient users of Internet resources and tools. The experience of network science projects suggests that comfort with technology tools per se may be much less an issue than comfort with the subject matter and data analysis at the heart of network science projects. Teaching teachers to use Internet browsers and spreadsheet software will not be enough; we need to make sure that they understand the science, the kinds of questions that can be addressed with data, and the analytic techniques that can address those questions with data. Moreover, teachers need to be able to make these difficult concepts accessible to their students. This book has far-reaching implications for the design of teacher professional development that will support effective educational uses of the Internet; those implications run counter to the narrower, technology-training path now taken by many districts and universities.

The second fundamental aspect of the authors' analysis is their argument that the kind of adult and peer support that can come from sharing data and interpretations are more likely to arise in the face-to-face classroom setting than over a network. Experience shows that few student exchanges in network science projects deal with scientific substance. Students are more likely to engage in social exchanges over the network and deal with data analysis and interpretation locally.

Certainly, the discussions that occur asynchronously over a network are more loosely coupled than those that occur in real time face to face. A student's question or conjecture sent out over the network is not likely to be answered immediately. In fact, more often than not it receives no response at all. Under such circumstances, it should not be surprising that students rarely attain new insights through their network interactions.

If the goals of network-based collaboration are to be attained, project participants need to develop a shared set of interaction patterns and norms conducive to reflection and intellectual growth. Because they have little experience with conversations about the analysis and interpretation of data, it is little wonder that few students engage in such conversations asynchronously over a network. Providing models of such exchanges and teaching students to be active participants in them, as the authors assert, are best done locally. Once such norms are established, project participants can reinforce the idea that they apply within the electronic realm as well as within the four walls of the classroom.

An elementary classroom I observed using the Computer-Supported Intentional Learning Environment (CSILE), for example, preceded use of this local-area-network technology by developing a set of norms for classroom interactions. Students were taught not just to avoid put downs, but to offer helpful, thoughtful responses. Their teachers stressed giving peers feedback that provides information or an idea to help the original speaker improve his or her work. The students learned that, although compliments are nice, they do not support improvement in the way that helpful, thoughtful comments do. Teachers found that their students extended the practice of providing helpful, thoughtful comments developed for face-to-face interaction to their work on the computer network.

Network science projects typically have devoted little attention to developing roles and norms for interactions. Without such norms, students feel little obligation to respond to the queries and conjectures of distant participants they have never met. The sense of mutual obligation is never established, and local priorities naturally take over.

In the end, I finished this book with two reactions. First, it reinforces my conviction that teachers' science knowledge and nontechnology skills are critical in making network science work for students. Second, despite technology having changed so drastically over the last 10 years, we have benefited greatly from the lessons learned in the early network science classrooms. Although the original vision was in some ways flawed, and these authors articulate and explain the nature of those flaws, that vision did inspire innovative classroom projects that generated a knowledge base on which later programs could build. The efforts of the early network science classrooms and project designers have made it possible for us to design programs using today's technology with a much better understanding of both the elements for successful classroom telecommunications and the role of data-driven inquiry in science education. As network technology matures and spreads, we will continue to draw on the lessons provided by these pioneering teachers and program developers.

*Barbara Means*
*Menlo Park, California*
*1999*

# Preface

E ducators are developing a variety of ways to utilize the powerful capabilities of the Internet to improve science teaching and learning for elementary, middle, and high school students. One of the best known and earliest of these efforts is National Geographic Kids Network—a curriculum that was initially developed by TERC and the National Geographic Society in the late 1980s with funding from the National Science Foundation. Since then, many other efforts have emerged that are similar enough that we refer to them collectively as network science curricula. Although each network science curriculum has its distinctive features, they all make use of online communities and shared sets of data to support students learning science. Whether the topic is acid rain (NGS Kids Network), environmental science (Global Lab), or butterfly migrations (Journey North), network science curricula have sought to enhance student learning through telecommunications.

Two research projects are responsible for the work reported here. Testbed for Telecollaboration (active from 1994–1998) and its predecessor, Alice/Collaborative Inquiry Testbed (active from 1992–1994), were funded by the National Science Foundation to support and research the implementation of network science curricula. As *testbeds*, these projects were designed to mesh with the efforts of partner organizations and develop common models and test conjectures about uses of technology in science education. Both Testbed projects were located at TERC, an educational

research and development organization in Cambridge, Massachusetts, whose mission is the improvement of mathematics, science,
and technology education.

The first goal of Testbed for Telecollaboration and its predecessor was to develop the technical infrastructure needed to serve
multiple network science curricula and to research the use of this
technology in classrooms. Testbed staff pioneered the web-based
server technology that supports many of these curricula
(Feldman, Johnson, Lieberman, Allen, & van der Hoeven, 1995)
and passed it onto some of its partner projects for use in other
web sites. The staff also designed and built a working prototype
for the telecommunications and data analysis tool that was
released as *NGS Works* in 1997.

The second goal, research, culminated in the writing of this
volume. Our research efforts included these four activities:

- working actively to support partner groups creating network science curricula, especially by providing assistance
  in data use and data analysis;
- learning from the experiences of these partners' efforts to
  develop, test, and implement network science curricula;
- fostering communication among the staff of these partner
  groups; and
- disseminating the knowledge arising from these endeavors.

Dissemination, for us, became integral to the entire research
effort. Indeed, our decision in the spring of 1997 to write a book
refocused our research efforts. The *what* emerged in the following
months as the six of us sifted collective experiences—foremost,
our experiences working and observing in classrooms as well as
what we had learned from solving problems with the staff of partner projects.

As the message took shape, the issue of audience became
clearer. As a result, this book is directed specifically toward the
type of individuals with whom we had been collaborating—namely,
project organizers, curriculum developers, researchers, and teachers who together are the pioneers in this unfamiliar landscape of
educational technology. As our work neared completion, we recognized that the perspectives and conclusions of our effort might also
be useful to a wider audience: school-based educational leaders,
policymakers, university-based faculty, and students enrolled in a

variety of courses examining issues of educational technology. The final chapter responds to the questions this larger audience is asking—and asking with some understandable urgency.

Our work raises troubling questions about the current political reality in which educational technology has emerged for many as the panacea for the array of problems plaguing our schools. At the urging of politicians and parents, schools nationwide are rapidly installing multimedia computers, high speed networks, and other technology. Most often teachers have little support as they struggle to use the technology and incorporate it into their work with students.

Those who spend time in classrooms might find themselves asking these questions: Are these technologies well suited to the needs of the teachers and students on whose desks they are being placed? What benefits can the public expect from schools that adopt technology? How can we know whether these expectations are being met? The simple truth is this: We are only at the early stages in learning how to incorporate technology effectively in schools. The nationally recognized Panel on Educational Technology clearly stated this point in March 1997:

> It is natural to ask what is currently known and what remains to be learned [about the use of computers in schools].... A review of the relevant research literature, however, suggests that although a substantial amount of very interesting and potentially significant work has already been done, we are not yet able to answer this question... the Panel believes such research to be critically important.... (p. 87, 91)

Despite a decade or more of technology use in schools, serious empirical studies that claim evidence of change are just now appearing (e.g., Wenglinsky, 1998).

Meanwhile, a reaction to the uncritical use of technology has surfaced in the press in the last 2 years. The well-publicized cover story in a national magazine on the use of technology in the classroom (Oppenheimer, 1997) as well as a publication on the effect of technology use on young children (Healy, 1998) sought to puncture the public's uncritical belief that computers in classrooms will, by themselves, help schools improve student learning. Both Oppenheimer and Healy questioned the costs and benefits of technology. Although remaining optimistic about the potential of educational technology to transform and improve educational practice, we agree that many schools have adopted technology without understanding—and committing to—the curricular and pedagogical changes that technology makes possible, and to the institutional changes that technology necessitates.

In our analysis, we have tried to debunk the idea that technology is a panacea. To see what a mixed blessing technology can be, one only has to look in many of the classrooms we have visited where teachers are struggling to master the technology while learning to teach new materials using unfamiliar pedagogies. However, we have also worked in classrooms where telecommunications has opened up avenues of inquiry-based teaching and technology is infused into many aspects of student learning. For the teachers and the students in these classrooms, teaching and learning without the enhancements and support of technology is hard to imagine.

This debate about the role, effectiveness, and costs of technology will be resolved neither quickly nor easily. Multiple questions about educational goals and alternative uses of limited resources hinder our ability to structure the debate. Nevertheless, our hope is that the research and theoretical perspectives on which we base our work will be of use to those educators who are pressing ahead (despite the debate) to develop sensible uses of technology. We remain optimistic that, given sufficient time for development, refinement, and implementation, technology will have a powerful impact on what and how students learn.

## RESEARCH BASIS

Over the last 4 years, the Testbed for Telecollaboration worked most closely with four network science curricula, providing services and direct support to Classroom BirdWatch, EnergyNet, Global Lab, and NGS Kids Network. (See Appendix A for brief descriptions of these network science curricula.) Other network science projects with which we cooperated in myriad ways include EnviroNet, Estuary-Net, Global Rivers Environmental Education Network (GREEN), Global Thinking Project, International Education and Resource Network (I*EARN), Journey North, and Kids as Global Scientists.

These network science curricula not only encompass great diversity but also possess the common elements of shared data and online communities. Several of these curricula, such as

Global Lab, were inspired by the early model of network science and maintain a strong resemblance to it. Others such as Journey North have pioneered substantially different approaches. In this volume, we explore some of the differences and the implications they have for the future of network science.

Although our work has been anchored in the experience of the Testbed researchers who worked closely with staff, teachers, and students of various network science curricula, it has also been informed by two additional sources of data. At the Network Science Conference, a diverse group of 33 curriculum developers, project organizers, teachers, researchers, and funders of network science curricula gathered at TERC to share their experiences and discuss the state of the art and future directions of network science. (See Appendix B for a list of participants at the Network Science Conference.) These discussions were provocative and far-reaching and inspired many of the ideas expressed herein, especially the lessons described in chapter 3. We are grateful for the contributions of the participants—for their thoughtful responses to an initial set of questions, for sharing their experiences at the conference sessions, which we taped, and for responding to the conference summary that we distributed afterward. In the months following the conference, we found ourselves returning frequently to these materials.

The Goodman Research Group Evaluation Report (1998) provided us with the second source of additional data. TERC contracted with Goodman Research Group for an external evaluation of Testbed for Telecollaboration during the project's third year (1996–1997). For this evaluation, GRG examined five different network science curricula. In conducting this comparative analysis, GRG examined three curricular projects that worked closely with the Testbed (Classroom BirdWatch, Global Lab, and EnergyNet) and two other network science curricular projects that were independent in their operation (Journey North and EnviroNet). The evaluators conducted interviews and surveys of teachers and project staff across all five curricula and supplemented these with data collected by each project whenever available. We found the data collected by the evaluators to be useful in our documentation of the conclusions of our work. (See Appendix C for the executive summary of the GRG Evaluation Report.)

Research, by its nature, is not neutral, and we do not intend that ours should be. Rather, we aim to be aware—and make our readers aware—of the beliefs that underlie the questions we ask and the methodologies we use. Foremost among our beliefs is the value we place on inquiry-based teaching and learning—a perspective enthusiastically supported in the national standards in science and mathematics. Our research is not designed to evaluate the value of inquiry-based approaches to teaching and learning. Rather, it examines the role that technology can play in fostering these approaches.

## ORGANIZATION

### Part I: State of the Art

The first three chapters describe the history and current practice of network science. Chapter 1, "Founding Vision of Network Science: Assessment," reconstructs the vision that emerged a decade ago among the group at TERC who imagined new curricula based on telecommunications capabilities that would foster inquiry-based science education. It is the nature of visions to motivate new efforts, and in this way the bold and inspiring network science vision was enormously successful. As often happens, the limitations of any founding vision become evident over time. We identify four aspects of the founding vision that have proved problematic.

Chapter 2, "Evolving Visions: Case Studies," presents the evolution and current state of three network science curricula: NGS Kids Network, Global Lab, and Journey North. The stories of these curricula illustrate the different ways that the network science vision has developed. We use these stories, which include the challenges faced by curriculum developers and project staff, to shed light on the founding vision identified in chapter 1 and point to promising new directions.

In chapter 3, "Lessons Learned," we look across the experiences of multiple network science curricula to identify what we and others have learned about using Internet resources to strengthen science teaching and learning. The seven lessons include priorities for curriculum development (e.g., "Look locally before globally") as well as advice on building infrastructure (e.g., "Design robust systems"). From these lessons, we identify and develop one of our key recommendations: The Internet should be used to broaden the scope of investigations that have begun with students studying phenomena locally.

## Part II: Looking Deeply

Despite what we have learned from the experiences of network science curricula, we see clearly that discourse and data, both critical to inquiry-based learning and teaching, need particular attention. The next two chapters extend our inquiry into network science by examining discourse and data in depth, using both empirical data and theoretical perspectives.

Chapter 4, "Promoting Reflective Discourse," examines how best to support class discussions. One goal of the founders of network science was that students, like collaborating scientists, would use the Internet to share data as well as ideas and would engage in serious discussions with one another. The evidence to date is not encouraging. Our research shows that online discussions in network science curricula are typically social in nature and not related to the substance of the science being studied. Based on our analysis of a transcript of a classroom discussion, we conclude that substantive online discussions are not likely to occur without a high level of support from the teacher and a classroom culture that values such discussions. We have difficulty imagining how to provide this kind of support online. We argue that it is less important where these discussions occur than that they occur somewhere. We conclude the chapter by discussing the type of curriculum-based support that teachers of network science need, but have not been getting, to promote reflective discussions in their classrooms.

Chapter 5, "Bringing Students to the Data," applies the insights of the mathematics education literature to the issues of data use in network science curricula. We begin with the observation that, despite our determined attempts, we have not been able to find classrooms in which students analyze in any depth the data made available to them. There are many reasons for this. Paramount among these is that students generally do not have in mind questions they want answered as they dutifully collect and upload data. We outline a set of principles for selecting tasks, data, and analysis tools appropriate for students. These principles are motivated and illustrated in two case studies: one of an expert analyst and the other of fourth-grade students being assisted by their teacher.

## Part III: Looking Forward

In the final chapter, "The Internet and Classroom Learning," we step back from the issues of network science to take a broader view. We focus on this question: How should the Internet be used—and *not* used—to support student learning?

We respond to this question in two complementary ways. First, we describe broad themes that have emerged from our work about the role of the Internet in classroom learning. Second, we look at how these themes are played out in a classroom. We present a vignette of a teacher we call Debra, who is actually a composite of teachers with whom we have worked. When we first see her, she is a good teacher who uses technology in marginal ways. We look again 3 years later after she has integrated online resources with her day-to-day teaching and observe how her teaching practices have changed as a consequence.

We conclude this work with a reminder that technology will not replace teachers. Rather, the power of these new technologies to give students both an overwhelming access to resources—experts, peers, teachers, texts, images, and data—and the opportunity to pursue questions of their own design increase the need for highly skilled teachers and forward-looking administrators.

### ACKNOWLEDGMENTS

TERC has served as a supportive, and sometimes feisty, research environment. We express our appreciation to many colleagues who contributed by sharing their own work, reading drafts, challenging ideas, and helping us avoid several egregious errors of fact and interpretation. Weaknesses that remain are certainly our responsibility and not theirs.

This volume reflects a decade of work at TERC and other institutions. Although we are unable to list all the individuals whose efforts supported our own, we express appreciation to those individuals whose efforts were especially important.

Our colleagues on the two Testbed projects supported and often inspired our work: Irene Allen, Dan Barstow, Ken Carlson, Chantal Eide, Michelle Gerrard, Eric Hilfer, Beverly Hunter, Charlie Hutchison, Lisa Johnson, Daniel Lieberman, Amy Neill, Bob Newby, Heidi Nyland, Kim

O'Niel, Steve Paris, Steve Schember, Susan Schoenberg, Steve Spodaryk, Robert Tinker, Johan van der Hoeven, Melissa Wahl, Joe Walters, Noel Wanner, and Bart Wise.

Our present colleagues at TERC, Barbara Sampson, Judy Vesel, and Teon Edwards, deserve special recognition for their willingness to read and react with great forbearance to parts of multiple drafts.

Teachers whom we have worked with and learned from. Among these, two in particular have helped shaped our thinking—Susan Wheelwright of the Fayerweather School in Cambridge, Massachusetts, and Bill McWeeny, a science teacher at Central Middle School in Quincy, Massachusetts.

Staff and teachers of EnergyNet in Illinois, Journey North in Minnesota, and NGS Kids Network and Global Lab in Cambridge, Massachusetts. Most of our data were collected with their cooperation. We learned much of what we now know through interacting with them in numerous conversations, e-mail exchanges, classroom visits, and workshop settings. Of particular note among these staff members are Joel Halvorson and Bruce Rigby.

Colleagues who read and reviewed an early manuscript. We appreciate in particular the insightful comments and support extended by Joel Halvorson, Jimmy Karlan, Marilyn McConachie, Theresa McMahon, Kathy Metz, Joe Polman, Margaret Riel, Cary Sneider, and Emily van Zee.

Staff at TERC who assisted in the design, production, and proof-reading: Jane Sherrill, Michelle Hlubinka, and Diane Hilser.

Our project officer, Nora Sabelli, at the National Science Foundation. Dr. Sabelli encouraged us to research how educational technologies actually get used in classrooms.

We thank James Karlan for permission to quote from his e-mail correspondence to National Geographic Society and TERC, dated April 4, 1995. His proposal for revising KGS Kids Network is cited in chapter 2.

We thank the publishers of the *Journal of Science Education*, Taylor & Francis, for their permission to include classroom dialogue in chapter 4 from J. Minstrell's class, quoted from van Zee and Minstrell (1997a).

We thank Bill Finzer at Key Curriculum Press for his permission to include his account of the data analysis session in chapter 5.

## AUTHORS

Alan Feldman, Ph.D., was the co-principal investigator on the first grant (Alice/Collaborative Inquiry Testbed) and principal investigator on the second grant (Testbed for Telecollaboration). Formerly a teacher and school head, he has been engaged in research and development at TERC since 1990. Most recently, he has been developing and evaluating systems of school-based support to assist teachers in integrating technology in their teaching.

Cliff Konold, Ph.D., served as the director of research for the Testbed for Telecollaboration in its final year. He is associate research professor at the Scientific Reasoning Research Institute, University of Massachusetts, Amherst, where he has worked since 1984. He is currently directing classroom-based research on how students reason about data in a networked environment.

Bob Coulter, Ed.D., worked on the Testbed for Telecollaboration staff during the 1995–1996 school year, and he has worked closely with the project since then. He has 12 years of teaching experience in the upper elementary grades and is currently an educational technologist at the Missouri Botanical Garden, where he is developing and managing an environmental monitoring project seeking to apply our research on network science curricula to the use of GIS software in schools.

Research associates Brian Conroy and Charlie Hutchison and research assistant Nancy London played important roles in the researching and writing of this book. Brian and Charlie currently work on a variety of research and development projects; both are former teachers of elementary and middle school students. Nancy has finished her graduate studies and is pursuing a career in public health.

Part I

# State of the Art

# Founding Vision of Network Science: Assessment

The 1980s was a heady decade for the development of technology. The decade began with the word *computer* assuming a whole new meaning. Until then, a computer was a large and expensive machine designed for computation and organization of data—a machine that needed to be programmed by highly trained experts. These units would be called *mainframes* today. However, the invention of the Apple II computer in 1977 and the IBM PC in 1981 effectively redefined the word. These new machines, initially called *desktop computers*, were then available relatively inexpensively to individuals. In short order, word processing replaced typing and spreadsheets became an indispensable tool for budgeting and accounting. The development of the modem and computer networks allowed information to be exchanged via telecommunications, and e-mail grew rapidly in popularity among the university community and later among businesses and individuals.

Some pioneering educators began exploring how these new technologies could improve teaching and learning. Network science—an innovative model of curriculum designed to foster inquiry-based teaching and learning—was one of the early applications of telecommunications technologies to education. The first section of this chapter reviews the development of network science, focusing on the ideas that shaped the model. Because much of this development was done at TERC, a research and development (R&D) organization in Cambridge, Massachusetts, the work of TERC figures prominently. TERC's efforts were not done in isolation, but reflected ideas unfolding at the same time in other parts of the country. The second section of the chapter traces these ideas—the roots of network science: science educators' belief that science is best taught through inquiry, the Science-Technology-Society movement, contemporary ideas about technology in education, and the newly emerging push toward school reform. In the third and final section, we offer an assessment of the founding vision of network science. Through our research, we have learned that some difficulties, which are typical of current network science practice in classrooms, stem from shortcomings in the original vision. We describe these shortcomings and make recommendations about how to remedy them. In subsequent chapters, we elaborate on these recommendations.

## THE FOUNDING VISION

Network science began with the simple idea of creating communication links among classrooms to share e-mail and data. Proposed as KIDNET and later renamed National Geographic Kids Network, the idea was developed through a collaboration of TERC and the National Geographic Society. Funded in 1986 by the National Science Foundation, NGS Kids Network made use of multiple new technologies—desktop computers, graphical user interfaces, modems, and computer networks—to enable the rapid exchange of messages between distant sites via telecommunications.

By 1986, the use of an electronic network to support writing in classrooms had already been pioneered in the QUILL project, Computer Chronicles News Network and InterCultural Learning Network, and FrEdMail. By giving students the ability to exchange text messages, these projects fostered collaboration among distant schools. Network science projects sought to go further than these pioneering electronic networks, giving students the ability to exchange data they had collected, thereby opening up the possibilities for cross-classroom collaborations to include shared data-rich inquiries. Some educators believed that, once these impressive new technologies were fully developed and in place, they would at last have the tools needed to make far-ranging improvements in science teaching and learning. Through network science curricula, they aimed to revitalize science teaching and learning from elementary school to the end of high school.

The group at TERC that developed Kids Network—Robert Tinker, Cecilia Lenk, and Candace Julyan, among others—documented their early ideas in a proposal submitted to the National Science Foundation in 1986 (TERC, 1986) and in articles published frequently over the next few years.[1] From their writings, we can construct the set of ideas that motivated NGS Kids Network. These ideas were developed further in subsequent network science efforts at TERC—most notably, the Star Schools project, Global Lab, Alice/Collaborative Inquiry Testbed, Testbed for Telecollaboration, and Kids Network: Leveraging Learning. Groups in other parts of the country were influenced by and, in turn, contributed to the development of these ideas, including the Beacon Project (Maine State Systemic Initiative), Classroom BirdWatch (Cornell Lab of Ornithology), Community Science Connection (Arnold Arboretum, Boston), EnergyNet (Illinois), EstuaryNet (Wells Estuarine Reserve, Maine), Global Thinking Project (Georgia State University), and the Nebraska Department of Education (Wetlands and Amphibians as Bioindicators curricula, jointly sponsored with the U.S. Environmental Protection Agency).

We refer to these ideas collectively as the *founding vision of network science*. Clearly, there was some evolution of the ideas over the last decade, but key ideas that have emerged across all the projects were firmly rooted in the early work of the group at TERC. Descriptions of these ideas follow (see Table 1.1 for summary).

Fundamentally, network science aimed to expand the classroom to a community of classrooms linked through telecommunications. This linking of classrooms had important implications for teaching and learning.

> Telecommunications expands the boundaries of the classroom, bringing together people with different perspectives, promoting collaboration. Students can explore relevant problems ... from geographically dispersed classes. For teachers, telecommunications can be an important way to decrease isolation and build support with other educators. (Lenk, 1989, p. 1)

For many network science curricula, this community of classrooms aspired to become a global community—one including students and teachers from all continents. The word *global* became a part of the names of many network science projects. A Pilot

## TABLE 1.1
## THEMES OF NETWORK SCIENCE PROJECTS

### Investigation of "real science" problems
- Students focus on real and compelling problems that are relevant to their lives.

### Students-as-scientists
- Students investigate problems not yet studied by scientists.
- Students learn scientific processes: framing investigable questions, conducting experiments, analyzing data, sharing results, etc.
- Student work is taken seriously by the scientific community because scientists have an investment in the outcomes.
- Students work within a cross-classroom community of practice.

### The role of data is critical
- Investigations require substantial data and the efforts of many investigators.
- Students learn to frame empirical questions related to these problems and answer them with the data.

### Constructivist learning
- Pedagogy represents a departure from traditional vocabulary-based, transmission model of teaching.
- Students learn by constructing their own understandings.

### Societal implications of science (Science-Technology-Society)
- Students need to be discerning about the ways in which science and society interact.
- Students advocate actions on the basis of what they have learned.

### Global learning community
- Students learn about different cultures and different environments through telecommunications and collaboration with peers.

### Pedagogical change
- Because the answers are not already known, the teacher must give up the role as the content expert with answers and serve instead as the expert on how-to-know.
- The teacher facilitates student investigations, acting more as coach than stage director.

TABLE 1.1 (continued)

Collaborative/cooperative learning

- Investigations inculcate the idea that science is a cooperative venture and emulate communities of practice in which scientists work.
- Collaborations in-class and online give students experience with collaborative work.

The affordances of the technologies are critical

- They promote collaboration and data sharing.
- They provide access to up-to-date information.
- They expand the boundaries of the classroom and decrease isolation.

---

Network for Global Education was first proposed by TERC in 1989, which became the Global Lab Curriculum.

Students, through network science curricula, would investigate relevant problems chosen by curriculum developers, project organizers, or students and their teachers. These problems would be authentic—that is, real problems, not yet solved by scientists, that students could study by analyzing data collected from dozens or even hundreds of classrooms. Their data would have scientific significance that data collected by one classroom, in one geographic area, could not have. For example, in the NGS Kids Network Acid Rain unit (1990, 1997), students collect data about acid rain in their own communities, submit these data to the central database, and retrieve the full set of data collected by hundreds of schools. When examined by students, the full set of data may reveal patterns of acidity in rainfall that no individual class is able discover by itself based on its own data. Over time, the grid of student measurements would have the potential to be much more finely grained than anything available to scientists, and this would become a potential resource for scientists to use.

Students were able to become scientific colleagues and collaborators; they were expected to submit data and make interpretations of the data, elaborate on the ideas of other students, offer critiques or challenges to these ideas, and question the meaning of terms. This approach was developed most intensively in the Global Lab Curriculum—an environmental science program designed to build research skills of students in Grades 8 to 10.

During the field testing of Global Lab, discussion forums ("Global Lab Voices") were set up for students and teachers to participate as colleagues across classrooms. Reflecting this new role, the original research of students and teachers was published in their own magazine, *The Planet: The Journal of the Global Laboratory Community.*

Network science also encouraged students and teachers to act on "the social implications of the scientific results" (TERC, 1986, p. B-2). The NGS Kids Network Acid Rain unit culminates with students looking for causes of acid rain in the pattern of industrial pollution and deciding what actions might be taken to decrease the acidity of rain and make rivers and lakes more habitable for fish and plants.

Network science advocates saw in new technologies a key to realizing this vision of authentic, inquiry-based science learning. Modem-based telecommunications opened up the potential for cross-classroom collaborations. Also important was creation of software that would support students and teachers in analyzing data. Inexpensive data analysis software was not available to schools, and what was available (spreadsheets) was limited in its functions and not appropriate for the kinds of inquiries being organized. The *Alice Network Software* (the prototype for *NGS Works*, 1997) was designed to give classrooms access to an inexpensive cross-platform software package—"an integrated suite of tools for word processing, graphing, mapping, and telecommunications" (Feldman & McWilliams, 1995), to support cross-classroom collaboration. With this software, students could exchange messages, create shared sets of data, and analyze these data (including graphing and display of data on simple maps). To work hand in hand with the *Alice* software, network science developers created server-based, automated, data-sharing software to handle the processes of data submission, consolidation, and retrieval.

The technical progress over this decade has been notable. In 1986, the Acid Rain pilot test utilized a scientist at the hub of network activity. This expert read and responded to e-mail, received data from individual classes, and sent out a consolidated set of data. Many TERC-supported projects in the early 1990s used the *Alice Network Software*, which adapted e-mail messages for purposes of data exchange. The system was cumbersome, however, and left students and teachers waiting to know whether their data submission had been successfully added to the consolidated data set. By late 1994, TERC began moving these projects to the emerging World Wide Web where there was potential for immediate feedback from the server and therefore better interaction by participants. TERC designed and built server functionality specifically to serve network science projects. This new web technology greatly simplified the submission of data, and students could submit data and then immediately view the data set consolidated from the data of multiple classes, including their own data. Students could also view and retrieve selected data subsets. In addition, the server enabled web-based discussions, which were designed to support teachers and students in solving technical or curriculum problems and to encourage an exchange of ideas about project-related content. These discussion groups served to give project staff greater interaction with participants and participants easier communication with one another. Finally, the server was a shared resource for all classes, giving up-to-date information on events and key dates as well as providing a library of shared documents and links to related resources.

The founding vision of network science was a bold one. Perhaps the most striking aspect of the vision, viewed from our vantage point a decade later, is not the global community of classrooms or the emphasis on relevant problems, but the role assigned to students in this curriculum model. No longer just learners, students were assigned the role of student as scientist. In the original proposal for Kids Network (TERC, 1986), the approach was referred to as a departure from both text-based instruction and contemporary thinking about inquiry learning:

> Student-as-scientist is even more motivating than guided-inquiry instruction. The answer for most inquiry investigations is known. ... KIDNET experiments, by contrast, have been chosen so that the answers are not known. (p. II-1)

Julyan (1991), former project director at TERC for Kids Network, wrote about her experience with network science, similarly emphasizing communications among classrooms and with scientists:

> The basic premise behind these curricula is that students can and should be scientists, that they can and should converse with real scientists about their work, and that computers can enhance this enterprise. Students conduct experiments, analyze data, and share results with

their colleagues using a computer-based telecommunications network. This collecting and making sense of data gives students the opportunity to experience the excitement of science that scientists feel. (p. 5)

Later still, Feldman and Nyland (1994) represented the vision of student as scientist this way:

> While collaborators may be geographically remote, they are tied together by a common problem or agenda. They may all be investigating the effects of ozone through a single approach (use of Global Lab's Total Column Ozonometer); or sites may be designing related experiments and requesting data from each other. The work of students in one classroom is fit into a larger effort of others, mirroring how scientists work. (p. 2)

In this model, the problems selected are real and engaging—ones for which scientists have yet to develop solutions. The curriculum aims to "connect elementary science with the real world outside the school," and content is "clearly related to real-life science issues" (TERC, 1986, p. A-7). Moreover, student work is taken seriously because the scientific community has an investment in its outcomes.

## ROOTS OF NETWORK SCIENCE

The original vision of network science, developed in the 1980s, was shaped by the availability of new technologies—principally the advent of inexpensive desktop computers and networked environments. The network science vision, however, also has roots in inquiry-based teaching and learning; the Science-Technology-Society movement, which was prominent in the 1980s; national reports urging a reform of U.S. education; and the new directions in researchers' thinking about the role of technology in learning and teaching (see Table 1.2). In this section, we summarize the influence of these intellectual threads on network science.

TABLE 1.2
ROOTS OF NETWORK SCIENCE MODEL

- Inquiry-based teaching and learning
- Science-Technology-Society movement
- National reports urging a reform of U.S. education
- New thinking about the role of technology in learning and teaching

## Inquiry-Based Teaching and Learning

The influence of the inquiry model of teaching and learning on network science is seen clearly in the original Kids Network goals. The first three of the goals stated:

- Let children do science through exploration, discovery, and testing.
- Make science challenging with age-appropriate activities that involve children in projects based in the world outside the classroom.
- Help children develop a flexible, problem-solving attitude toward experience. (TERC, 1986, p. A-1)

These goals represent a rejection of traditional vocabulary-based transmission pedagogies. The vision of network science builds on the understanding (developed most notably by Jean Piaget, Jerome Bruner, and, more recently, Seymour Papert) that students learn through constructing their own knowledge. The goals also acknowledge the importance that Dewey (1910, 1929, 1938) placed on problem solving and reflective inquiry as mechanisms of learning. In the spirit of the project method of the Progressive Movement, these goals also recognized that students should be solving problems of genuine interest and relevance to them, using concrete materials "in a purposeful activity in a natural setting" (Kilpatrick, 1918).

Network science is also indebted to the innovative science curriculum reforms of the late 1950s and 1960s.[2] Like the reforms of the progressives before them, these projects aimed to exploit students' natural interests and curiosity. The goals of these projects were to model scientific inquiry and develop problem-solving skills. These projects emphasized hands-on activities and open-ended questioning as a means to develop the process of discovery learning—that is, observing, questioning, comparing, collecting data, and building theories.

Network science modified the practice of inquiry in the classroom by adding the new goal of student as scientist, which had one clearly differentiating quality:

The answer for most inquiry investigations is known, and learning happens when students "puzzle out" the answer. KIDNET experiments, by contrast, have been chosen so that the answers are not known. (TERC, 1986, p. A-1)

In network science, students would be investigating areas that scientists are still exploring.

## Science-Technology-Society Movement

Another influence on the network science vision of school science was the Science-Technology-Society (STS) movement, which was a major force within science education in the 1980s. Within the STS framework,

> Science education is defined, then, as the discipline concerned with the study of the interaction of science and society, i.e., the study of the impact of science upon society as well as the impact of society upon science. Their interdependence becomes a reality and the interlocking concept for the discipline. (Yager, 1984; cited in Bybee, 1987, p. 668)

In this view, exemplary science programs should focus on social problems and issues and emphasize student decision making, local and community relevance, and cooperative work on real problems (Yager, 1984).

These ideas are reflected in many network science projects. A focus on environmental problems is common; it provides a context for students to do research about their own communities using the immediate environment as the laboratory. Students investigate real problems that affect their own communities and the planet, and can submit recommendations to policymakers. In this way, students learn to understand their role as stewards of the environment and its natural resources.

## National Reports Urging a Reform of U.S. Education

In the early 1980s, the National Commission on Excellence in Education (1983) told Americans,

> Our Nation is at risk. Our once unchallenged preeminence in commerce, industry, science, and technological innovation is being overtaken by competitors throughout the world ... the educational foundations of our society are presently being eroded by a rising tide of mediocrity. ... If an unfriendly foreign power had attempted to impose on America the mediocre educational performance that exists today, we might well have viewed it as an act of war ... unthinking, unilateral educational disarmament. (p. 1)

The political hegemony that the U.S. wielded in the post-World War II era had eroded, and Americans began to see themselves as vulnerable to economic competition.

With this report, the nation embarked on a series of efforts to examine and resolve the perceived weaknesses of the educational system. The dire prognosis of U.S. education and the need to make fundamental changes helped set the stage for the development of network science as a new curriculum model. In addition, two early themes of the school reform movement prepared the way for network science. First, the school reform movement called for the use of just-emerging computer technology throughout the curriculum (although how was left altogether vague). Second, the movement advocated not only the use of new curriculum materials but also new approaches to learning. Network science curricula clearly responded to both these themes.

## New Thinking About the Role of Technology in Learning and Teaching

Network science was developed in the context of a changing understanding of the role technology would play in school teaching and learning.

Many early educational uses of computers involved computer-assisted instruction (CAI). The model of learning was fundamentally a behaviorist one, relying on predetermined sequencing and repetition for learning. During the late 1980s, many school districts made significant investments in a variant of CAI, often called *interactive learning systems*. Subsequent research studies on this use of technology found little value compared with traditional modes of instruction (Collins, 1996). Drill-and-practice software is a contemporary descendant of this genre of educational technology and makes use of the same basic ideas about student learning.

Koschmann (1996) looked at the history of educational technology over the last two decades and subdivided the innovations into two distinct paradigms. The first, which he called *Logo-as-Latin*, marks an important break with the earlier theories of *what* and *how* students should learn, and it builds on a constructivist set of understandings. Rather than computers teaching a set body of knowledge to students, Papert created the *Logo* language (1980) to enable students to control the computer through mastering a simple programming interface. A similar emphasis on students' learning through their own actions characterizes microcomputer-based laboratories, games such as *Logical Journey of the Zoombinis* (Broderbund, 1996), and simulations such as *SimCity* (Maxis, 1994) and its successors.

The second paradigm, Computer-Supported Collaborative Learning (CSCL), builds on the constructivism of the first paradigm and adds a focus on the social context of learning. In this paradigm, students are viewed as members of communities with common goals, and technology supports the work of the community. Early work in this genre would include e-mail exchanges such as QUILL (Bruce & Rubin, 1993), Computer Chronicles News Network and InterCultural Learning Network (Mehan, 1985, 1989; Riel, 1985), and FrEdMail (Levin, Rogers, Waugh, & Smith, 1989). The development of the Internet has allowed for the development of much more advanced CSCL environments than these earlier programs. Besides network science projects, more recent examples of CSCL environments include multiuser virtual environments (MUSEs and MUDs; e.g., MicroMUSE at GTE/BBN), CSILE (Scardamalia & Bereiter, 1996), as well as network science curricula.

There is significant overlap between many of the qualities of these two paradigms. Collins (1996) used the term *interactive learning environment* to encompass both of them, and he listed the following capabilities of such environments (1996): realistic situations, simulation, animation (i.e., ability to see processes that are otherwise not observable), expert advice (presented just when the learner needs it), video, diverse knowledge sources, multiple representations, testing hypotheses through modeling, scaffolding, and reflection. These capabilities enable interactive learning environments to "support learning in ways that schools [elsewhere: human teachers] cannot easily provide" (see Table 1.3).

Because these learning environments support a constructivist and collaborative approach toward learning and teaching, it is not surprising that many of these elements are evident in the network science projects. Of the elements of these learning environments, network science projects typically make use of realistic situations, expert advice, diverse knowledge sources, multiple representations, testing hypotheses through modeling, scaffolding, and reflection. These elements are seen in the case studies presented in chapter 2.

TABLE 1.3
CAPABILITIES OF INTERACTIVE LEARNING ENVIRONMENTS

- Realistic situations *
- Simulation
- Animation
- Expert advice (presented just when the learner needs it) *
- Video
- Diverse knowledge sources *
- Multiple representations *
- Testing hypotheses through modeling *
- Scaffolding *
- Reflection *

* indicates elements typical of network science projects

*Note:* Adapted from Collins, 1996.

## ASSESSING NETWORK SCIENCE

As bold and inspiring as the founding vision was, the shortcomings of this vision have become more and more evident. As difficulties in network science projects were identified, project organizers and researchers initially attributed them to inadequate technology or teachers' and students' lack of understanding of the technology. Even after technological problems were ameliorated, however, many of these difficulties persisted. Therefore, with the benefit of hindsight—and a decade of experience—we have come to understand that some of these difficulties stem from weaknesses in the original vision.

Several sources highlight these issues. Based on the work of the Alice/Collaborative Inquiry Testbed at TERC with its partner projects, Feldman and Nyland (1994) reported problems that were apparent across a number of network science curricula. This study represented a broad look across programs; a second study (Karlan, Huberman, & Middlebrooks, 1997) provided a detailed account of the use of one curriculum, NGS Kids Network, in 11 classrooms at seven schools over 9 months.

Many of the issues outlined by these research studies were echoed by project organizers, curriculum writers, and teachers at the Network Science Conference (which the Testbed staff convened in November 1997) and in the evaluator's report on the work of Testbed for Telecollaboration (Goodman Research Group, 1998).[3] They were additionally substantiated by the authors' observations in classrooms and informal conversations with teachers participating in a number of network science curricula. In the last year, outside evaluations of network science curricula have become available and point to some of these same issues (e.g., SRI's evaluation of Global Lab Curriculum—Young, Haertel, Ringstaff, & Means, 1998).

The more we know, the more we are enlightened by the subtleties affecting the effective use of technology in support of inquiry-based teaching and learning. The development of productive models for educational technologies demands that we learn from our initial attempts and look carefully at the complex realities of supporting students and teachers in the hard work of learning.

In the remaining section of this chapter, we point to four aspects of the network science vision that have proved difficult in practice over the last decade. These problems include:

- Supporting teachers
- Identifying the community of learners
- Making data meaningful
- Engaging students in productive inquiry

Our discussion includes recommendations as to how to approach each of these problems. We elaborate on these recommendations in subsequent chapters.

## Supporting Teachers

Although the network science vision attempted to build on the work of an earlier generation of educators advocating guided inquiry, its proponents did not adopt all of the ideas put forth. Most significantly, the role of the teacher was not given much consideration in the founding vision of network science. Curriculum materials often assumed an unrealistically high level of pedagogical experience and knowledge on the part of teachers, and they offered inadequate support for teachers who were just starting to use network science curricula.

It is only the teacher who can set the stage in the classroom for students to engage the ideas of others and thereby fosters the kind of thoughtful, reflective discussion that characterizes learning; through questioning, the teacher helps students develop their own understandings further. The experience of network science projects points to this crucial role that the teacher must play in supporting student inquiry and the importance of greater support for teachers. Network science projects have only recently begun to give the required attention to these new roles for teachers. By contrast, developers of an earlier generation of guided inquiry curricula elaborated the crucial role of the teacher from the start. Their role was described extensively by Elementary Science Study developers Jerome Bruner (1962, 1971) and David Hawkins (1965a, 1965b, 1974).

In chapter 4, we discuss the problem of providing better support for teachers in the context of providing support for reflective discourse.

## Identifying the Community of Learners

Having the technological capability for widespread telecollaboration is not enough to ensure that it will happen. Just because a class can share resources and expertise with other classes does not mean that cross-classroom collaborations will develop and that the databases constructed will be used for question generating, analysis, and interpretation. In fact, participants in network science projects typically do not achieve a high level of cross-classroom collaboration.

We believe that the problem lies in the relative emphasis placed on telecollaboration in contrast to the natural community of learners based in the classroom. Network science holds out the promise that a learning community can be constructed online—as the virtual community formed by all the classes working together—and that this community will have greater potential to encourage learning than the classroom. We now believe that it is critical to identify the classroom as the primary community of learners in which the dialogue among students takes place. In this setting, students have the ongoing day-to-day and face-to-face interaction with peers and a teacher through which the norms and skills of inquiry can be learned and continually supported.

We believe there is a powerful role for the virtual community: It is best utilized as a way to enrich the primary, classroom-based community—that is, to provide new and contrasting contexts in which to understand experiences. These ideas are pursued in greater depth in chapter 4.

## Making Data Meaningful

Network science focuses on the use of student-collected data to study topics that are considered relevant to students' lives. However, the data collected are often too complex for students to comprehend. Because these data tend to be cumbersome, abstract, noisy, or inaccurate, the data sets are difficult for students and teachers—even experts—to analyze. As a consequence, when classes successfully collect the required data, we see little use of the data for analysis and few contributions to online discussions about the data.

Data sets need to be simple in design, and the purpose of cross-classroom sharing and consolidation must be clearer than it has been in many network science curricula. Archival data sets should be used to supplement data collected by students. (These archival sets can be based on data collected by students in previous years, but they must be cleaned up before distribution.) Most of all, teachers and students need support in learning that data analysis is more than generating graphs. At its heart, data analysis is a process of creating hypotheses and using data to test or reformulate hypotheses, creating and structuring data that test these hypotheses, searching the data for insights, and making and critiquing arguments based on the data. Network science projects have not yet incorporated this perspective on data analysis and thus fall short of their goal of students analyzing data. These ideas are elaborated on in chapter 5.

## Engaging Students in Productive Inquiry

Many network science projects have not lived up to their potential to involve students in productive inquiry. First, the network science model of curriculum typically constrains classrooms by imposing rigid schedules for data submission and exchanges. The low level of completion for many network science projects—which, according to Karlan et al. (1997) was less than 50% of classes in one project submitting data—may reflect teachers' inability to fit the real lives of their classrooms, punctuated by school events and holidays and snowstorms, into the schedule demands of many network science projects.

The consequence of a rigid schedule, however, is even more significant than a low level of completion. Karlan et al. (1997) pointed out that the data-sharing model in use by NGS Kids Network, shaped by the goal of collecting and exchanging data across large numbers of classrooms, is not consistent with often-stated characteristics of inquiry practices. The program requires a single pace of activities for participation. For many classes, this required pace allows little time for students to reflect, revise their work or personal theories, and probe other students' thinking, or for classes to explore divergent but relevant inquiries. This finding about NGS Kids Network is typical of other network science curricula.

Aiming to coordinate work among classes, many network science projects are constrained by centralized schedules. To refocus science learning on inquiry, teachers and students need flexible schedules to allow questions to be pursued in greater depth. Without such flexibility, the potential of the curriculum to support student inquiry is greatly diminished.

(Karlan et al.'s study of the strengths and weaknesses of this curriculum inspired the current revision of the NGS Kids Network curriculum. This evolution of NGS Kids Network curricula is the basis of a case study outlined in chap. 2.)

Second, network science encourages the use of real scientific and social problems to spark learning, focusing on the importance of investigating questions for which the answer is not known. However, this emphasis on questions for which the answer is not known and the questions (and data) are of genuine interest to scientists excludes the possibility of students investigating concepts that may be well known to scientists but no longer of interest to them. Because such concepts are still unknown to students and potentially of great interest, they offer a scientific excursion through which students can reliably have successful and powerful learning experiences. For example, students might investigate phenomena as simple as why some objects float—a topic that is unlikely to be of any interest to scientists.

Linn (1995), participating in an informal review of network science curricula, described this problem from a cognitive perspective:

> If ... we focus too much on problems of concern primarily to research scientists we run the risk of teaching students concepts and principles that they lack opportunity to practice and are therefore prone to forget.

Julyan (1988) experienced the difficulty in creating activities under such constraints when she was directing the development of NGS Kids Network:

> While a number of activities make terrific inquiry-type classroom experiments, a large percentage of those activities are not suitable for a national network of classrooms or are not of use to scientists. The challenge in our curriculum is to find the delicate balance of educationally significant experiments that will be successful in both a classroom and a national network and that are of interest to the scientific community. (p. 6)

Looking across some of the projects inspired by the network science vision, we fear that the balance has been struck on the side of real science to the detriment of "terrific inquiry-type" experiences for students.

Finally, the challenge of engaging students in productive inquiry is complicated by the thinking encouraged in the shorthand metaphor of student as scientist. The phrase has power and utility in emphasizing the constructivist perspective that students should not be treated as the proverbial empty vessels to be filled, but rather as curious beings interested in the ways the world works, able to learn from one another, and capable of helping to shape their own learning.

However, this metaphor falls short of capturing the complex reality. It does not take into account the stages by which students grow into the complex intellectual and social roles of a scientist. The metaphor of student as scientist has encouraged network science projects to overlook some crucial questions of students' developmental levels (e.g., what behaviors of scientists can students productively model at each level as they grow in their intellectual understanding of science concepts and in their ability to assume social roles?).

The National Science Teachers Association has dealt with this issue in its various standards publications. For example:

> Although all students have the capacity to inquire, that capacity changes and becomes more sophisticated as students mature and gain

experience. Younger adolescents explore questions with trial-and-error experiences and experiments, and they are introduced to testing by learning about variables and establishing controls. As adolescents develop cognitively, they become capable of using more formal thinking skills, such as the manipulation of several variables and using abstract thinking. (National Science Teachers Association, 1998, p. 7)

For example, 10-year-olds are immensely curious and eager to talk about how they see the world—qualities that might be labeled as those of a scientist. Unlike scientists, however, they have little experience with the concept of *acid* beyond (at best) some familiarity with the word. Any curriculum that concerns acids would need to present at length the experiences from which some aspects of the concept of acid might be developed, such as the interaction of acids and metals or acids and living systems. However, the curriculum would not be able to present the underlying chemical structures of acids for which the 10-year-old is not at all prepared. Furthermore, despite the readiness of 10-year-olds to learn to respect evidence and struggle with fair testing, they still lack the ability to define a hypothesis or control variables in an experiment by themselves. These skills require careful structuring of curriculum and support from the teacher (see, for example, Driver, Guesne, & Tiberghien, 1985).

The documents that capture the founding vision of network science provide scant reference to developmental issues in students' learning. The vision draws deeply on the constructivism inherent in thinkers like Piaget, but gives much less attention to Piaget's equally compelling evidence for developmental learning stages. Network science projects have sometimes struggled to identify content appropriate to students at a given level, and too often have chosen content and modes of learning that are overly sophisticated for these students. As a result, too much reinterpretation of the curriculum has been left to the teacher.

The lessons learned by network science projects over the last decade, described in chapter 3, define the role of technology in engaging students in productive inquiry.

Technology has inspired for many the compelling idea of students transcending the limits of their classrooms and schools. The earliest version was that teaching machines (CAI) would replace teachers. A more recent version, part of the founding vision of network science, was that communities and resources on the Internet would create entirely new learning contexts.

The example of network science urges greater caution. Too often the developers of network science have relied on technological answers to the design problems that arose. Moving from undifferentiated e-mail to web-based threaded discussions was one such change, and creating better tools for data analysis was another. However, the technology was not able to solve the problems of how to give teachers the skills and time needed to participate productively in online discussions or how to support teachers and students in learning the requisite skills to make use of the improved data tools. Technology will no doubt have a role in solving these problems, but the role will be only as one component of a broad-based plan for improving teaching and learning. No curriculum can effect meaningful change without the presence of a broader context to support these changes. This statement is especially true with programs like network science curricula where teachers are widely dispersed and therefore not able to benefit from ongoing, face-to-face support.

The importance of a strong local context for implementing substantial educational change is made by Young et al. (1998):

> However, as yet, technology does not provide the same intensity as having a mentor come to one's classroom, discuss the learning objectives and approach for a lesson, observe the lesson, and provide critical feedback on what went well and what could be improved. Although one could imagine a way of using technology to accomplish this . . . such communities are very difficult to build and sustain. . . . (p. 95)

The experience of other technology-rich educational innovations is instructive. Fitzpatrick (1997) summarized the experience to date of researchers looking at the integration of the geographic information systems (GIS) software into classrooms.

> However, our experience shows that there are two characteristics that, far above all else, predict a teacher's ability to use the tool effectively: the teacher's willingness to engage in his/her own unpredictable exploration and the willingness to allow students this same opportunity. Far more influential than even the presence or absence of

powerful hardware, the teacher's modeling of "a lifelong learner and thinking explorer" predicts whether certain students will get the chance to use GIS. Thousands upon thousands of children are in schools that are technologically rich but explorationally poor, while some fortunate scores of their brethren, even in sites with just one computer, are encouraged to be thinking explorers, following the model of their teacher ... sometimes even ahead of their teacher in exploring new territory. (p. 33)

Technology has a vital role of supporting inquiry-based teaching and learning. However, our experience with network science curricula over the last decade points to the importance of technology being carefully and thoughtfully implemented within a broader context that supports these same changes, including revised curricular goals for students and significantly greater opportunities for teacher professional development. Technology, after all, is only one component in fostering a "teacher's willingness to engage in his/her own unpredictable exploration and the willingness to allow students this same opportunity."

# Evolving Visions:
# Case Studies

T hree network science projects—National Geographic Kids Network, Global Lab, and Journey North—encompass a range of approaches to fostering inquiry-based teaching and learning. Case studies of their evolution give insight into the challenges that curriculum developers face in creating and improving network science curricula.

These case studies convey the distinctive elements of each curriculum. In addition to describing how each curriculum is used in classrooms, we elaborate on the evolution of each project—what problems emerged, what solutions were tried, and what was learned. We give particular attention to documenting changes to each project's approach to supporting inquiry teaching and learning. Finally, we look at the current challenges that face each project; these challenges include uses of new technologies, transitions in their modes of dissemination, and plans to expand the number of teachers who have used these projects' curricula.

The founding vision of network science, described in detail in chapter 1, continues to evolve. These case studies document the variety of ways that the original vision has changed over the last decade.

NGS Kids Network is an appropriate starting point for these case studies because it is the original network science curriculum, first published in 1989. It has been widely distributed; thousands of elementary teachers have been introduced to telecommunications. In 1997, each of the NGS Kids Network units for elementary grades was revised and four additional units were published for the middle grades. In the fall of 1999, NGS began releasing a second major revision of all the Kids Network units, including a substantially new structure to the units and alignment of the Kids Network units with other web-based NGS educational products. The case study summarizes how developers used new technologies to provide enhanced support for student inquiry and, through the NGS School Publishing division's education web site, planned to make NGS Kids Network units more easily and inexpensively accessible to teachers.

Global Lab applied the network science model to the high school level and created the year-long Global Lab Curriculum. While focusing on ecology, the curriculum aimed to develop more generalized student research skills, culminating with their use in extended investigations. The case study captures efforts by developers at TERC to find the right balance between process and content, to define a significant role for the Internet in supporting the development of students' investigative skills, and to release a commercial version of the curriculum in 2000.

Journey North represents a significantly different approach to network science from that of NGS Kids Network and Global Lab. Participating teachers, primarily in elementary schools, are provided online and print resources designed to help teachers create their own units of study. This approach contrasts with most other network science projects, including NGS Kids Network and Global Lab, in which teachers are given detailed, sequential curriculum guides. Journey North's approach enables teachers to participate incrementally as they develop comfort with the content, pedagogy, data, and online scientists. The case study focuses on the distinctive approach developed by the Journey North staff, the key role played by the funder, Annenberg/CPB, and Journey North's plans for expansion.

A comparison of the key features of these three projects is summarized in Table 2.1.

## NGS KIDS NETWORK[4]

*A veteran Kids Network teacher, Marcy Danton,[5] and her fourth-grade class field tested the Acid Rain unit; this new revision included much greater use of web resources. Children had access to the Internet on a single computer in the room and on the 17 computers in the computer lab from which they were able to access the Acid Rain web site.*

*Compared to the earlier (pre-web) version of Acid Rain that she had used in previous years, Mrs. Danton observed that the revised unit extended the experiences of the students in significant ways. For example, the earlier Acid Rain curriculum asked students to test the pH of local rain. To perform the tests, children collected rain. This activity involved them in researching, designing, and building rain catchers to place outdoors. In the revised unit, students were able to prepare for this activity by viewing some rain catcher models on the Acid Rain web site. These models were used to stimulate student discussions about how to design and construct their own devices. When the students built their own rain catchers, they incorporated new elements as well as those elements seen on the Internet or mentioned during classroom discussions.*

*The Acid Rain web site also offered children links to Internet resources that afforded them opportunities beyond those available in the print version. A link to the Miami Museum of Science's pH Meter allowed children to simulate a test of the pH of a variety of materials. Some materials, such as Liquid Plumber, posed a special thrill due to the implied danger of the substance. Real-time data sites, including live weather, and archived databases were available for children to view and analyze as well.*

*The revised unit offered other opportunities to Mrs. Danton and her class. As part of the field test, Mrs. Danton posted messages for others to read. In this way, she developed a professional relationship with Joan Lourdon, a field-test teacher in New Hampshire. Mrs. Danton and Mrs. Lourdon shared curricular ideas, developed a project together, and arranged a classroom visit when Mrs. Lourdon was in the Boston area.*

TABLE 2.1

SUMMARY OF THREE NETWORK SCIENCE PROJECTS

| Attribute | National Geographic Kids Network |
| --- | --- |
| Grade level | Originally developed for Grades 4–6; expanded to Grades 3–9 in 1997 revisions. |
| Availability | Web-based units scheduled for released starting in the fall 1999. Previous versions discontinued. |
| Project type and structure | Traditionally an 8-week interdisciplinary science curriculum; web-based units give teachers greater flexibility of use. |
| Content | Interdisciplinary science with an emphasis on the nature of scientific inquiry. |
| Data sharing | Data shared using *NGS Works* software through either a modem or high-speed Internet connection. Beginning in fall 1999, data sharing and retrieval through web-based forms. Data posted on web site for retrieval by other classes. |
| Data analysis tools | *NGS Works*, a software program with mapping and graphing capabilities. Version 3.0 runs in a browser window. |
| Internet use | Starting in fall 1999, most student and teacher materials available online with links to external web resources. Through an electronic bulletin board, support for class-to-class and teacher-to-teacher communications. |

| Global Lab: An Integrated Science Program | Journey North |
|---|---|
| Grades 8–10. | Nonspecific; most users are in the upper elementary and middle grades. |
| In press, to be published by Kendall/Hunt Company in January, 2000. | Online at www.learner.org/jnorth. Teacher manual (optional) from Annenberg/CPB. |
| Full-year course with five units. Curriculum begins with Becoming a Global Community and culminates with Extended Investigations. | Resource materials on migrations and signs of seasonal change: • tracking locations • local sightings • information/ interpretation by experts |
| Interdisciplinary science, with an environmental theme. Covers four science disciplines: biology, chemistry, earth science, and physics. | Environmental science, focusing on wildlife migration and other seasonal change. |
| Data submitted on the Internet using web-based forms. Data posted on web site for retrieval by other classes. | Submission of data to Journey North via web forms. Data posted on web site for retrieval by other classes. |
| Locally chosen. | Locally chosen; many phenomena have a map representing the data provided with the data set on the web site. |
| Student projects use web resources to extend inquiry. Extensive use of web-based collaboration, online publishing, and e-mail. | Background information on each species and on signs of seasonal change. Teacher discussion area; questions submitted to experts; optional e-mail to other schools to pose questions about local data. |

NGS Kids Network was originally funded in the mid-1980s by the National Science Foundation (NSF) as a collaboration between TERC and the National Geographic Society (NGS); the NSF has maintained a long-term commitment to supporting revisions and extensions of the curriculum through continued grants to the collaborators to cover the costs of curriculum development, field testing, and evaluation.

NGS Kids Network was a response to the national calls for better and more relevant science education described in chapter 1. The intention of the collaborators was to develop and market curriculum using telecommunications. The curriculum would reflect a project-oriented approach and involve students in investigations. In contrast to prescribed "cookbook" exercises, these investigations were to:

- focus on real-world problems rather than contrived or context-free activities;
- involve students in cooperative learning, both with classmates and with remote classes; and
- encourage interdisciplinary studies rather than science alone. (TERC, 1986, p. A-1)

The curriculum was also developed to embody an approach called Science-Technology-Society (STS). This approach aspires to develop scientifically literate students who apply their scientific knowledge and skills to solving ordinary, everyday problems. Reflecting these roots, the culminating activity of the original Acid Rain unit (1990) challenged students to propose solutions to the problems of acid rain and write letters advocating these solutions to decision makers such as politicians and corporate executives.

During the 1996–1997 school year, NGS Kids Network units for Grades 3 to 6 was used in more than 4,300 classrooms; since the inception of Kids Network, NGS estimates that 60,000 classes and 2 million students in all 50 states and in 52 countries have used these curriculum units.

In 1999, 10 years after the publication of the first unit, NGS began releasing a second major revision to the original Kids Network curriculum. This revision aimed to support more open-ended student inquiry and to make use of advances in technology. In addition, these revised units linked scientific literacy more closely to literacy approaches that are typically more familiar to elementary teachers; for example, teachers were encouraged to integrate factual scientific writing and oral presentations—skills emphasized in the English Language Arts Standards—into their lessons. The new units, still called NGS Kids Network, are referred to in this volume as *web-based units* to distinguish them from the earlier versions of the materials.

The descriptions and analyses that follow cover various versions of NGS Kids Network curriculum units, including the web-based units. Unless otherwise indicated, the analyses were based on the teacher's guides for the Acid Rain curriculum unit. The referenced teacher's guide may be the NGS Kids Network 1990 version, the NGS Kids Network 1997 revised version, or the 1999 preproduction version for the web-based unit. Many descriptions generally apply to all units, and differences among the units that highlight the evolution of the developers' thinking are explicitly pointed out in the description that follows.

## The Curriculum in the Classroom

Over the course of its first decade, NGS Kids Network units were originally organized as a series of structured lessons over a 6- to 8-week period in which students learned about the topic being investigated and collect relevant data to analyze locally and exchange through the network. For example, in the Acid Rain unit, students in each class wrote descriptions of their local community, including factors that influence the formation of acid rain (e.g., local energy sources and pollution). Students also collected local rainwater and measured its acidity. The students' measurement of the acidity of rainwater (pH) and the latitude and longitude of the school (called the global address) formed the network data which were then sent to the central server and made available to all classes participating in the study. Students downloaded the set of network data from all participating schools and analyzed it using specialized software. This software created a map with the data superimposed, displaying visually the geographic patterns in the acidity of rain. Students were encouraged to search for and explain patterns in the data, drawing on the background knowledge developed in the previous weeks.

The curriculum was designed so that students first analyzed local data, then data collected by a small group of classes (team). With this experience, they turned to searching for patterns in the data submitted by all classes participating in the Acid Rain unit.

To support students and teachers in their use of data, NGS released *NGS Works* in 1997. *NGS Works* marked a significant improvement over earlier Kids Network software and other data analysis software designed for elementary and middle schools students. Modeled on similar multi-function products, *NGS Works* enabled students to use a single software application to send and receive e-mail, write and illustrate reports, retrieve and submit data, and analyze data. A noteworthy feature, one not typically found in educational software, was the ability to look at data geographically, that is, represented on a map.

## Project Evolution

An in-depth evaluation of NGS Kids Network curriculum (Karlan, Huberman, & Middlebrooks, 1997) concluded that NGS Kids Network was successful in introducing many teachers and students to hands-on science activities and in developing science process skills. However, the researchers concluded that the project frequently did not achieve its goal of fostering inquiry-based teaching and learning. They characterized the activities of the original NGS Kids Network units as "algorithms, in which the topics, problems, and strategies are mainly selected by the program and teachers" (p. 281). The units were fast-paced so there was little time for student reflection, discussion, or questioning. Important aspects of inquiry, such as students formulating their own questions, were absent. Evaluators reported that, according to some teachers, the telecommunications component actually inhibited inquiry, and they speculated that slow technology and the high attrition of classes in the team were contributing factors.

The study also found that many teachers were still immersed in what the evaluators refer to as *didactic* and *experimental* paradigms as opposed to the *constructive* paradigm to which NGS Kids Network aspired. Thus, although Kids Network developers intended that the hands-on activities would lead to discussion and analysis, teachers implementing the curriculum focused almost all of their time and efforts on the mechanics of doing the experiments, virtually omitting scientific processes such as the posing of questions and analysis of the data to find answers. Karlan et al. concluded that the NGS Kids Network curriculum was generally too constraining and did not allow students to develop their own investigations.

In private correspondence with NGS and TERC, Karlan proposed a plan for significant revisions to the existing material:

> These [proposed materials] hang from a . . . pedagogy I believe [is more aligned] with current teaching and learning theories. It is a pedagogy that I believe students will be more engaged with, by having more learning opportunities to problem solve, [and invent] problems, behave like scientists, analyze data, and cooperate in ways . . . that generate knowledge and understandings about phenomena. (Karlan, 1995)

Karlan's memo sparked NGS and TERC to review and revise the existing units. The results were two revision cycles: the 1997 revisions incorporating new software and some changes in pedagogy and the revisions that were released beginning in 1999 that restructured the units and moved them fully onto the Web. The web-based units were significantly different from the original versions. The most obvious changes were reflected in the thorough integration of new technologies and the resultant restructuring of the units. Equally important changes were made through carefully planned changes in pedagogy.

*Integrating New Technologies.* The original NGS Kids Network predated the availability of the Internet in schools. The revised units made extensive use of the Internet for providing student access to curriculum materials and distributing materials to teachers at lower cost. New software was also published which used the browser as the basic interface for the NGS data analysis software.

The most notable change in the web-based units was that all student materials were made accessible online (Fig. 2.1). Using their browser, students moved easily from the online curriculum materials to other web sites, for example, sites showing recent data collected by scientists about the acidity of rain across the United States (Fig. 2.2) or describing the effects of acid rain on living and nonliving things. According to the developers, field test data demonstrated that students used this additional information to develop better understanding of the concepts that are the focus of the unit.

**FIG 2.1. Students access online materials that link directly to activities.**

Screen capture courtesy of TERC

[1999, September 8]

Use of Internet technologies also provided NGS with the opportunity to make teacher materials accessible to more schools. Teachers were able to register to participate in NGS Kids Network units at no cost and had the option of free use of web-based materials or purchase of additional materials at moderate cost. NGS printed teacher materials as binder inserts produced at lower cost than the earlier materials. The only materials that teachers were required to purchase (if not available locally) were materials needed for activities (in the case of the Acid Rain unit: pH strips and pH color charts).

Reflecting their move toward a more integrated use of the Web, *NGS Works 3.0* (released in the fall of 1999) was designed for students and teachers familiar with web tools. It incorporated the functionality of the earlier versions of *NGS Works*, but instead of remaining a separate application, it evolved into a set of applets that run in a browser window. Just as *NGS Works* created a single user interface for an earlier generation of NGS Kids Network users new to software, *NGS Works 3.0* created the same consistency of interface for the generation of Kids Network users who were technologically more savvy and whose world was becoming increasingly web-based.

A version of *NGS Works 3.0* (applets) adequate for the curriculum units was also planned to be available for download at no cost. However, to use a full-featured version of *NGS Works*, teachers had to purchase the software.

*Restructuring the Units.* The online learning environment enabled developers to create a new structure for the units. Rather than offering prescheduled sessions, NGS Kids Network offered teachers the flexibility to register online and participate in any unit at any time—a significant change from earlier versions. Classes were no longer assigned to a team of classes, nor was there a timetable to link the team activities. Rather, classes could choose to establish partnerships with a small group of classes within the larger community of students doing the unit and communicate via e-mail. Curriculum materials could also be used in multiple ways: Teachers could follow the full curriculum or select particular activities. Because curriculum materials were linked to specific learning standards, teachers were free to select specific lessons based on their goals. Teachers were able to schedule their class activities as they chose, request data collected by many classes for purposes of data analysis, and communicate with other classes through a bulletin board.

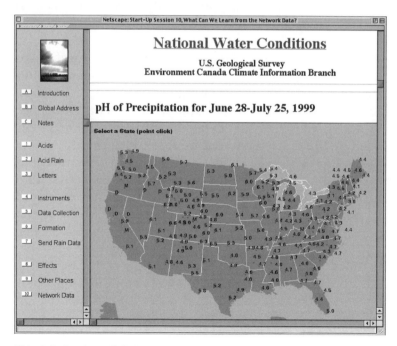

**FIG. 2.2. Students link from the Acid Rain unit, Activity 10, to authentic data collected by scientists about the pH of rain.**

h2o.usgs.gov/nwc/NWC/pH/html/ph.html [1999, August 3]

In addition to these major and easily observed changes, the revised NGS Kids Network incorporated significant (if more subtle) changes in pedagogy, reflecting NGS and TERC's experience in working with teachers and broader changes in the world of education. These included alignment with national standards, design of new models of web use, better support for classroom discussions, and expanded student use of data.

*Aligning With National Standards.* The movement for educational reform nationally resulted in the creation of national standards for most disciplines. Once these standards emerged, NGS decided to align the Kids Network units with them. The standards relevant to Kids Network were the National Science Education Standards, National Geography Standards, and—added with the 1999 revision—the National Standards for the English Language Arts. An unexpected benefit of this attention to the standards was that NGS Kids Network found a new way to reach teachers: Teachers who were more comfortable with language arts than the sciences were more motivated to embrace the core science content when the links to language arts were clearly developed and made explicit to them.

*Designing New Models of Web Use.* In the revised units, student materials were put online with links to external web sites; these sites provided rich and informative background material, simulations, and access to current and archived data. Developers aimed to select web sites that related directly to the questions being posed by the curriculum and were reliable, interesting, and conceptually appropriate for students. In creating their model for student use of the Web, they were addressing the concerns raised by researchers about students' ability to use web resources productively. Soloway and Wallace (1997), for example, observed that students using search engines to locate research materials were often overwhelmed by the number of entries located and ended up frustrated in their search for useful sites. The web-based units avoided this problem by structuring students' work through online student materials (Figs. 2.1 and 2.2). Browser frames kept the unit outline in front of students as they went through a sequence of activities, seamlessly moving to external sites and back. In effect, students were given direct access to specific, developer-chosen sites and an easy method of return; in this way, students avoided the potentially frustrating process of web searching. Although the external sites were selected by the developers, students pursuing locally developed inquiries were free to use their browser to access other Internet sites as their inquiries evolved.

*Supporting Classroom Discussion.* In the web-based units, the curriculum developers placed greater emphasis on the role of discussion in the classroom and encouraged teachers to allow students to share their ideas about the topic at hand. New goals were added for the web-based Acid Rain unit:

- engage in conversations and express opinions that are scientifically and technologically informed;

- pose and evaluate arguments based on evidence and apply conclusions from such arguments. (NGS, 1999, p. 7)

Because many teachers find such open discussions very difficult, the developers supported teachers in leading effective classroom discussion through materials in the teacher's guides. In Session 4 of the Acid Rain web-based unit, How Will Our Instruments Look? the concluding discussion follows a classroom activity in which groups of students design and build rain collectors and gauges. The teacher's guide suggested that teachers do the following:

Ask a representative from each group to explain how features of the group's instrument will result in accurate measurements. Have students discuss the merits of each design. (TERC, 1999, p. 72)

By describing what to focus on (in this case, the merits of each design), these directions illustrated the emphasis of the curriculum on strengthening classroom dialogue. Clearly, the revisions of NGS Kids Network were an important step. However, our analysis of classroom discourse in chapter 4 suggests that support for discourse in the classroom requires much more professional development than can be provided in a teacher's guide. Thus, although the developers made important changes, schools and districts have to offer staff development coordinated with the curriculum if the goal of substantive discussions in the classroom is to be realized.

*Expanding Student Use of Data.* Starting with the 1997 NGS Kids Network units, students had access to more and different kinds of data sets than were available with the original units. Besides the data sets collected by other NGS Kids Network classes in the same school year, two other types of data sets were available to teachers and students. First, archival data sets from former Kids Network years were available for the first time (*NGS Works* supports the use of these data sets). Second, the web-based units took advantage of current data (including real-time data) available through the Internet (see Fig. 2.2). To analyze these data sets, students used *NGS Works* or data tools embedded in a particular web site or analyzed the data set by hand.

Several sessions focused on data analysis. Students were supported through instructions on choosing a question, making a prediction, and locating suitable data to analyze:

> Choose a question to investigate as a class or in small groups.
>
> Is the mean (average) pH of rain lower (more acidic) in some areas than in others? . . .
>
> What is the pH of rain in areas surrounding the place that reported the lowest pH (highest acidity)? . . .
>
> What is the pH of rain in areas surrounding the place that reported the highest pH (lowest acidity)? . . .
>
> Write the question you chose on a sheet of paper. Make a prediction about what you think you will discover. Then write your prediction below the question. Also write one or two sentences to explain your prediction.
>
> Make a map to help you answer the question. Look at the map and discuss what you see. Remember to ignore the zeros. Use your discoveries to decide if your prediction is correct. If it isn't, try to figure out where you went wrong. (TERC, 1999)

Thus, the developers recognized that students must be guided through the data analysis components of the inquiry process, moving from suggested questions to their own questions. They were assisted in doing this by the curriculum materials and with the active support of the teacher.

## Current Challenges

NGS Kids Network is one of many offerings NGS publishes for schools; starting with the 1999 revisions, Kids Network was aligned with the other educational initiatives within the NGS School Publishing division. Reflecting this larger change, NGS

Kids Network became a feature on a new educational web site; instead of being a stand-alone product, it became a part of a larger set of web-based offerings. This integration had the advantage of presenting to teachers a more coordinated effort; however, it also posed a challenge of continuing to meet veteran Kids Network teachers' expectations for the product.

Through the years, NGS attempted to incorporate new advances in technology as appropriate. Through these changes, NGS took advantage of the growth of the Internet and increased capabilities of the web to enhance the program with the goal of reaching more teachers and substantially lowering costs to schools. The challenge for NGS was to ensure a smooth transition to this new environment and find effective ways to support teachers. The transition had to be made rapidly enough so as not to lose the large cadre of teachers who have used NGS Kids Network curriculum units for years, while at the same time finding ways to bring in new teachers. Most importantly, the challenge was to maintain the long-standing strength of NGS Kids Network—presenting multidisciplinary curriculum materials that engage students and teachers in scientific inquiry.

This case study suggests how the original NGS Kids Network evolved by responding to new understandings of how students learn and making use of emerging technologies. Developers adjusted the curriculum in an effort to provide greater support for the type of reflection, questioning, and exchanging of ideas that are appropriate challenges for elementary grade students. They moved away from the structure of 6- and 8-week sessions, and teachers were allowed to enroll in any unit at any time or to select only specific activities when those activities were appropriate. The developers also integrated the Internet's large repository of information and interactive resources to support students' inquiry learning and used the Internet as an efficient, low-cost distribution medium for educational materials.

The NGS Kids Network curriculum is characterized by a sophisticated level of science concepts for elementary students. The unit topics reflect the original vision of engaging students in scientifically significant inquiry. Topics such as acid rain, solar energy, and nutrition certainly qualify as important areas of scientific concern, but without thorough classroom-based support, these concepts may be problematic for students. In Piagetian terms, most 8- and 9-year-olds are *concrete operational* and require a base of experience to work successfully with concepts such as *acidity* and *energy*. Without such experience, students' abilities to interpret data sets about acid rain, for example, may be limited. This is especially true when the students are encouraged to extend their inquiries with their own questions—a notable stretch when the concepts themselves are not ones with which students have had much prior experience.

(Note: Starting in 1999, NGS planned to label its curricula units with more limited grade levels; the Acid Rain unit, for example, was targeted at Grades 5–6.)

NGS Kids Network units reflect the perspective of *student as scientist.* This metaphor, although attractive in many ways, must be interpreted in light of the developmental stages of the children participating. This requires the teacher to make decisions, carefully informed by her knowledge of her students, about how to implement the curriculum. Reflecting this necessity, the activities of 8-year-olds using a NGS Kids Network unit should look quite different from the activities of 12-year-olds doing the same unit. It was left to teachers, however, to provide much of this important accommodation to the level of their students.

## GLOBAL LAB[6]

*Mr. O'Leary, a veteran teacher of Global Lab, used the curriculum in several of his classes in a middle school. He set up an environment in his classroom in which 20 or so terraria used in Global Lab activities lined the classroom walls. Each terrarium was maintained by an individual student. A separate section of the large classroom was partitioned off with a couch and chairs and a wet model of the GL pond site. The actual pond site was behind the school building. On the most recent data collection day, students went outside to the pond to collect samples of water and measure temperatures, pH, and depth of the pond. Although it may have appeared to a casual visitor that it was a very informal activity, the students worked with a great sense of purpose as they went about making their measurements. Once back in the classroom, they talked about the data they had collected and worked on their model pond. Because Mr. O'Leary had been on sabbatical the previous quarter, the model pond site had been neglected, so these students were re-creating it. They had brought in mud from the pond outside, had planted some plants and pebbles, created a dam, and put in a fish. Algae had already formed, and the students were speculating about other organisms that might form. (Adapted from Goodman Research Group, 1998)*

The main goal of the Global Lab Curriculum was for students to develop inquiry and analytical skills that can be applied to future science learning within the content framework of environmental science. The curriculum grew out of a vision that viewed new telecommunications technology as a tool for enabling "kids around the world to participate in global studies, and by so doing, learn about science and intercultural cooperation" (TERC, 1989). The environmental theme has proved to be motivating to students and successful at fostering interdisciplinary study (Lieberman & Hoody, 1998).

The curriculum focused on developing students' research skills and encouraging them to work as real scientists. In the words of the proposal writers, the curriculum was

an attempt to support the restructuring of science education by making student-based research a real and vital part of school science. (TERC, 1991, p. 1)

The Global Lab view of inquiry was strongly influenced by the student-as-scientist metaphor, with students' work designed to be similar to that of professional scientists. Students were to collaborate with fellow students worldwide to design and conduct experiments, exchange data from their own experiments, and analyze the full set of data in pursuit of answers to questions of current scientific interest. As with NGS Kids Network and other curricula, however, these ideals needed to be tempered by the students' developmental levels—namely, the available knowledge base and sophistication of the students involved.

The final Global Lab Curriculum was the direct outcome of three phases of work, each funded by a separate grant from the National Science Foundation to TERC. The first two phases, A

Pilot Network for Global Education (1990–1993) and The Global Lab Curriculum (1993–1995), resulted in the creation of curriculum modules. The final phase (1995–1997) resulted in a full-year environmental science curriculum for students in Grades 8 to 10. This project story focuses on the prepublication version of the curriculum entitled *Global Lab: An Integrated Science Course.*

## The Curriculum in the Classroom

Global Lab aimed for students to become adept at devising research questions for any topic regardless of content. To support this goal, the curriculum progressed from structured, whole-community activities to student-defined investigations. In the first four units, the goal was for students to develop the kinds of learning attitudes the American Association for the Advancement of Science (AAAS) *Benchmarks for Science Literacy* refers to as "habits of mind" (AAAS, 1993). These included students' willingness to participate in investigations, scientific curiosity, openness to exchange, and honesty in collecting data.

With these skills in place, students worked with greater freedom to pose interesting and viable research questions and devise ways to test them. In the final unit, Extended Investigations, students chose their own research questions, sought collaborators within the Global Lab community, and devised their own research plans.

The prepublication version of Global Lab marked a more careful use of the student-as-scientist metaphor than was used in the past. Previously, Global Lab accentuated the parallels between the work of students and scientists. Through experience in classrooms, developers realized the limitations of the metaphor. In the final version of the curriculum, students made the connection between their learning and the work of scientists in very specific ways. For example, in one unit, two groups conducted their own research and then switched roles; each group replicated and built upon the previous work of the other group, with the goal of understanding that their respective work was both interrelated and interdependent.

Throughout the year, the curriculum materials emphasized that there is no single scientific method. To support this perspective, the curriculum included interviews with GLOBE scientists and others who illustrated the diverse approaches scientists take in conducting their research.

## Project Evolution

As Global Lab moved from pilot test to field test to its first published version, there were many issues which emerged; these issues may be of interest to others writing similar curricula.

*From Modules to a Year-Long Curriculum.* Global Lab staff had hoped that the project would evolve with a strong professional development component. From years of experience in organizing and administering the project, developers found that combining technology with inquiry learning was overwhelming for teachers. Furthermore, all support and orientation for Global Lab teachers occurred remotely—because of the geographic range of the classes—thereby exacerbating this difficulty. Thus, project developers, wishing to improve the implementation of the curriculum, proposed the "Global Lab Implementation and Adaptation Project" in August 1994 to design and conduct workshops. When the proposal was not funded, project developers' plans for professional development were of necessity limited to curricular materials and the teacher's guide.

The final phase of the Global Lab project was funded to convert the curriculum modules into a full-year course for publication and widespread dissemination. This change was a response to teachers' claims that they could effectively implement the program only through a yearlong curriculum. In practice, comparatively few of the field test teachers used the curriculum as a full-year course. Instead, most used it as a component of or a supplement to a larger course (Young et al., 1998).

*Balancing Support for Inquiry Skills and Content Knowledge.* In the past, the curriculum was more heavily weighted toward inquiry and less toward content. This emphasis was based on the developers' beliefs about good classroom practice. In the final field test version, responding to feedback from teachers, administrators, and parents, developers placed more emphasis on content. This issue produced a constant tension in the development process, as the Global Lab team sought to create the right balance of inquiry process skills and content knowledge.

Developing effective means of helping students learn the content of the curriculum has also presented challenges to the developers. The curriculum included numerous readings and resources (some online—see Fig. 2.3) to support the content objectives in each unit, but the developers were concerned that these materials adequately serve as the primary texts for the course. In addition, they believed that some of this material is more sophisticated than much of the Grades 8 to 10 target audience could handle (Peake, 1997).

*Curriculum Design.* Developers struggled with two major design issues: curriculum organization and matching schools' technological capacity. Each of these issues challenges most network science programs.

First, developers had to choose the best way to organize the Global Lab Curriculum. After balancing the merits of a definite structure against the merits of merely suggesting options, the decision was made to provide a clear structure—recognizing that teachers could then adapt it to their needs. In practice this is just what has happened, with many teachers picking and choosing components to fit their curriculum (Young et al., 1998). As with NGS Kids Network units, a highly sequenced series of investigations was intended to model how a network science curriculum could be implemented. Those more comfortable with the pedagogic model and technology could then adapt it to their needs. (This structured model stood in marked contrast to the approach taken by Journey North described in the next section.)

**FIG. 2.3. Global Lab Curriculum uses online readings and resources.**

globallab.terc.edu/

workspace/resources/

landUnit.html

[1999, September 9]

Second, developers had to decide whether to write a curriculum to meet the classrooms' present or future technological capacity of classrooms. Leigh Peake, a project director of Global Lab (1996–1997), acknowledged that the final curriculum was written with a vision of what the technological capacities of future classrooms would be like. For example, classrooms were expected to telecommunicate, exchange data, and start building classroom web sites right from the first days of the project.

Global Lab staff members were aware, however, that for the purposes of the final field test (1997–1998), these expectations were not yet realistic ones, given the current level of access to computers and the Internet in most schools. While schools generally have increasingly greater access to the Web, teachers have sounded a cautionary note. In the October 1997 survey, responses indicated that using web technology remains problematic; even teachers who identified their computer access as "good" or "great" indicated that the availability of Internet access and time to use it were still obstacles.

*Use of Data.* As with NGS Kids Network, Global Lab developers intended that students examine their local data before performing any global analyses. After analyzing their local data, students then compared their local phenomena with that of other schools worldwide and drew conclusions about global phenomena. These data exchanges were posted on the web board around activities presented in the curriculum.

In the initial units, which focus on the importance of observation, the data are mostly qualitative (sights, sounds, impressions, patterns). In later units, data consist of measurements taken of various environmental impacts on a school's study site. These data were generally numeric expressions of the biochemistry and biophysics of the air, soil, and water (e.g., measures of biomass and concentration of nitrogen and phosphorous in a site's soil).

Global Lab staff consciously tried to go beyond the traditional science curriculum's emphasis on data collection and presentation by emphasizing data analysis. The goal was to instill in students an understanding of how to use data for interpretation and the importance of questioning the data's quality and variability (Peake, 1997).

To support this process, increased guidance was given for teaching the mechanics of data analysis. Curriculum materials included an activity that outlined the features of different types of graphs, a section in the teacher's guide on analyzing data, and suggestions and guiding questions for individual data analysis activities. For example, the following instructions came from an activity analyzing light and temperature:

Students can start by determining the patterns and the gradients of how each parameter varies from one location to another. How much variation is there? Have students identify the highest and lowest temperature they detected and the greatest and least light intensity. Can students detect a relationship between light intensity and temperature? (TERC, 1997, p. 282)

After students developed skills in analyzing local data, classes were encouraged to work with the network data. Developing an appropriate support structure for classes to participate in this networked environment proved to be quite a challenge. Throughout the development of Global Lab, staff members attempted to find productive ways to structure data sharing. When the curriculum specified definite dates for submitting data, many more classes submitted data. For an early data-sharing activity in the final field test (Fall 1997), all schools were asked to collect data as close as possible to solar noon on the autumn equinox. This activity was successful in eliciting data submissions from 46 classrooms out of approximately 80 participants; it produced the desired result of a large sample of geographically diverse data. Although this experience was successful, the project developers realized that there were potential drawbacks to this kind of scheduled activity. Similar to the experiences of many NGS Kids Network teachers, classes sometimes felt constrained or rushed by having to meet submission deadlines, thereby not doing justice to the deliberative nature of inquiry.

Another ongoing question was whether to have students work with the raw, original data that are posted in the community databases, or cleaned up versions of the data. Developers recognized the problems inherent in having students work with unwieldy tables that often contain complex data. One consequence was that few classrooms actively manipulated or commented on the data contributed by peers on the network. The challenges of working with data are discussed more fully in chapter 5.

*Use of Telecommunication.* From the beginning, Global Lab attempted to use technology to build a community. In the first field test, classrooms created materials that described themselves in words, pictures, and voice recordings. These were sent to the developers, who in turn distributed a CD-ROM with the collection of these self-descriptions. The availability of the Web has changed the nature of this activity, but not its goal. Activities in the first weeks of the 1997–1998 field test focused on each class' construction of web pages. (Although as noted previously, technology obstacles limited the number of classes that were able to participate in this activity.)

Another key goal of the Global Lab Curriculum was for student collaborators to play a significant role in planning and implementing extended investigations, choosing collaborators, and posing their own research question. The vision for use of telecommunications to support this goal was that students would begin to build relationships with other students in the community, both within local sites and among networked classrooms, so that later in the school year they would feel comfortable posting their research and soliciting collaborators.

According to project developers, they searched for the best way to allow student collaborators to shape the project throughout the research process—enabling students to identify collaborators and engage in the give-and-take necessary to determine the research question. For the final field test (1997–98), the Global Lab Online Workspace (GLOW)[7] was used for data sharing. This authoring tool was designed to enable Global Lab staff members to create projects for which classrooms submit data. Later in the year, the space enabled students to publish their Extended Investigations online and encourage collaboration. During the field test, a significant number of student projects were published via GLOW, but there was little indication that other schools have looked at the projects—let alone collaborated.

Designing an infrastructure to support teacher use of telecommunications proved to be equally challenging. Prior to the Web, Global Lab telecommunications consisted of multiple listservs. In their mailboxes, teachers found messages from their colleagues and project staff about specific content areas (e.g., Aquatic Ecology, Weather, and Climate) or support issues (e.g., a project bulletin board, a discussion of data and relevant issues, the chat of a teachers' room). Many teachers reported being overwhelmed by the number of e-mail messages in their mailboxes daily, and few had the experience to sort out the messages of greatest interest or relevance.

When a more complete use of the Internet was incorporated into the curriculum, messages were sent through a web-based discussion forum (Global Lab Voices), which was compartmentalized into content issues, teachers' discussions on specific topics, and student sharing. Teachers could then choose more easily how to spend their available time. The plan for publication, however, was that teachers and students would communicate via a single e-mail listserv, with all messages archived on a web site. This reflected feedback received from teachers who did not want to have to log on to send and receive their messages, as was required by Global Lab Voices.

## Current Challenges

The challenge for the Global Lab Curriculum is to make the transition from grant funding to commercial stewardship. During the years in which Global Lab materials were developed, the project leadership spoke with dozens of potential publishers, many of whom expressed some interest. However, innovative materials were considered risky in the marketplace, and many publishers were not interested in publishing and supporting the curriculum. Additionally, TERC staff reported that publishers also felt ill-equipped to support the telecommunications components which, in the Global Lab Curriculum, were woven throughout the units and were essential to the use of the materials.

In 1999, Kendall/Hunt Publishing Company accepted the challenge of commercially publishing the curriculum with its extensive telecommunications component. They planned to make the print materials available in the spring of 2000, with telecommunications scheduled to come online the following fall for the start of the new school year. Kendall/Hunt anticipated building its market starting with the teachers who were involved in the numerous field tests of the curriculum, then attracting significant numbers of middle and high school science teachers by marketing directly to schools with access to computer and Internet technology. Despite the risks that accompany innovative materials, Kendall/Hunt believed that a commercially viable market existed for the Global Lab Curriculum. "Teachers now have technology in their classrooms; Global Lab gives them a reason to use that technology" (Al Vincent, 1999).

Once the publishers attracted a viable base of teachers, they needed to provide support for many teachers for whom the inquiry approach and the technology were unfamiliar. They planned to do this in ways similar to their support for other products. For professional development, they planned to offer inservice and summer workshops for teachers; to respond to questions from teachers, they planned to mobilize their staff, their sales representatives, consultants, and the writers (TERC) to post questions and answers on an electronic bulletin board. However, they did not anticipate that the revenues from the project would enable them to create staff positions devoted exclusively to support for Global Lab teachers.

Similar to NGS Kids Network, Global Lab faced a number of challenges in the last decade and evolved in response to the experiences of teachers and students. Several of the themes explored in this case study recur in many network science curricula: challenges relating to curriculum structure, the use of technology, the quest for community among distant classes, and support for effective data analysis. The last two of these are explored in much greater depth in chapter 4 (Promoting Reflective Discourse) and chapter 5 (Bringing Students to the Data). In addition, Global Lab is facing the transition from grant funding to commercial stewardship.

## JOURNEY NORTH[8]

*The Franklin School, a small, suburban elementary school, had been working with Journey North for 2 years. The principal, Ms. Manning, learned of Journey North from a National Science Teachers Association publication. Several teachers at different grade levels adopted parts of the program, working toward gradual implementation of Journey North in ways that supported the school's curriculum requirements as well as state and national standards. Ms. Manning's support of this longer term view of change has been instrumental in helping teachers integrate technology effectively.*

*Working in conjunction with a local scientist who studied eagle populations in the area, students in Mr. Fillmore's sixth-grade science class studied the relationship between eagle migration and weather patterns. Mr. Fillmore also used the monarch migration portion of Journey North with his students. The first-grade teacher was doing a unit on butterflies and was looking for an interesting project for his students that included use of the Internet. The first and sixth graders became "butterfly buddies"—the sixth graders gathering information from the Internet and bringing it to the younger children. The older children also helped the first graders with their drawings and stories and kept track of their own Internet work through journals. (Adapted from Goodman Research Group, 1998)*

"A Global Study of Wildlife Migration" was how Journey North described itself. The study of wildlife migration was a key component in the project; the lack of any reference to technology in its description communicated the low priority that project staff members placed on the use of computers in the project. The focus was clearly on the natural phenomena and how they can be studied locally. As Joel Halvorson, Journey North staff member, noted, "We have found that success has a lot less to do with the technology, and a lot more to do with good teaching strategies and an ongoing engagement of kids in pursuits of local inquiry" (Testbed for Telecollaboration, 1997). However, the Internet component was invaluable because it provided context and extensions to locally grounded investigative work.

Many teachers found that the real value of Journey North was the way in which it captivated and built students' natural interest in animals. This initial engagement provided the leverage for studying many complex scientific phenomena. On a formal level, Halvorson described the project as a study of the "function of various interrelated natural systems responding to an increase in energy from the sun to re-create the annual rebuilding of the food chain" (Testbed for Telecollaboration, 1997). Clearly these were not the terms an elementary or middle school student would have used, but students gained an appreciation of seasonal change and migration by participating in the program. Depending on how an individual class chose to become involved, natural phenomena could be compared in the same season or comparisons could be made between current data and the same phenomena in years past.

Teachers' investment in the project was quite high, as shown by the 94% reenrollment rate from 1997–1998 (Leichtweis, 1998). Respondents to a Journey North survey cited two factors as the most valuable components in the project: the basis in real-time events and the connection to practicing scientists. Journey North Director Elizabeth Howard (1998) quoted one teacher:

> Journey North was a real project for my students. They felt ownership of it because they were studying real animals with scientists, not just reading about them. They learned a great deal and so did I. My students loved this project.

## Curriculum in the Classroom

*Use of Data.* Journey North supported in-depth inquiry by providing students with access to up-to-date information on the arrival of spring in the northern hemisphere. Weekly or biweekly updates on each species (e.g., manatee or monarch butterfly) and sign of spring (e.g., "leaf-out" or "ice-out") provided current data. Depending on the phenomena being studied, these updates may have included local sightings, latitude and longitude points from satellite tracking, maps, and comments from the online expert. Students used these data to track spring's progress as represented by animal migrations, plant changes, and seasonal climate and weather shifts.

To help students make sense of the data, two basic supports were used—an extensive manual (available in print and online) and a group of approximately 60 online experts. First, the teacher's manual alerted teachers to some of the key issues affecting the species' migration and suggests avenues for inquiry. For example, a loon inquiry (Donnelly & Wiley, 1997) could be structured around the suggested questions of whether loons will fly over large areas without water or how this year's migration compares with those from previous years. In many cases, suggestions were made in the manual as to how productive inquiry may be guided through reference to the current data and the archives available online. The eagle page suggested:

> Students will participate in an on-line guessing contest and predict the location of this eagle's nest. To guide their guess they'll analyze

satellite data collected during the springs of '94, '95, '96, and '97 as well as banding data from other New York eagles. (Donnelly & Wiley, 1997, p. 121)

*Support for Inquiry.* Besides these topic-specific supports, there was a series of lessons on inquiry in the manual. Some of these lessons are generic pieces on latitude and longitude and making careful observations, but some attempted to develop skills in areas that most projects do not explicitly treat, such as differentiating the role of firsthand and secondary information, verifying the accuracy of data, and forming theories. Although these were critically important skills in an inquiry-based classroom, a single lesson in one of these areas was insufficient to develop inquiring students. How these issues were actually dealt with on a daily basis in the classroom was much more important in determining how much students learn about inquiry.

The second major support for student inquiry was the provision of online experts. The scientists who reported on each species for Journey North were all volunteers, although a "very small" honorarium was generally paid at the end of the season. This was noteworthy because the extent of involvement among these experts was clearly more than a token form letter or two during the project. Typically, these experts provided periodic summaries of satellite data and biweekly commentary on the data. They also responded to several hundred questions posed online by students.

Howard attributed the success of this approach to the willingness of the field biologists to provide detailed, regularly scheduled commentary about what is being observed. Although the experts also answer many questions posed by student participants, Journey North organizers saw this work as being of secondary importance. The key function provided by the experts was to keep the students in touch with the scientists' work studying natural phenomena. For the students to make sense of the data and participate in the flow of the inquiry, the implicit mentorship in scientific inquiry offered in the commentary, which accompanies many data sets, was deemed of great value by many teachers. This area was one in which Journey North sets itself apart from other projects. For example, Highway to the Tropics provided only the latitude–longitude data sets and generic lesson plans about raptors without the benefit of regularly scheduled expert commentary.

## Project Evolution

Journey North began in 1993 as part of a Will Stegar expedition to the Arctic. Elizabeth Howard, who later became the founder and director of Journey North, advanced the idea that students would be more fully involved in the project if they could connect in a personal manner to the study of the Arctic. Migration of Arctic animals was seen as the vehicle for this connection; Howard built on student interest in these animals, their travels, and related environmental issues.

The Annenberg/CPB Math and Science Project decided to fund the project as part of the foundation's larger effort to support inquiry-centered teaching and student-directed science learning. Besides offering financial support, Annenberg/CPB provided marketing, promotional, and technical assistance. The initial funding was in place in December 1994—in time to support the project's work with the spring 1995 migration. The initial press release, which was addressed to "Students Across North America," described the program's vision and the resources that it offered to teachers and students:

Beginning on Groundhog's Day 1995, students will travel northward with spring as it sweeps across the continent of North America. With global classmates and state-of-the-art computer technology, they will predict the arrival of spring from half a world away.

Students will witness the wonders of migration as they travel "live" with some of the world's most accomplished wild adventurers—bald eagles, monarch butterflies, sea turtles, songbirds, peregrine falcons, caribou and loons—on the annual journey their ancestors have traveled for generations.

Up-to-the-minute news about migration will be exchanged between classrooms as students report observations from their own hometowns. The dramatic migrations of several Journey North species will be tracked by satellite. News about these journeys will travel from the animal's transmitter to an orbiting satellite and then directly into the classroom via the Internet. This revolutionary technology will give students a bird's eye view of the remarkable challenges faced by individual animals as they migrate.

Linked to classrooms from the tropics to the Arctic, students will conduct interactive, comparative studies of the natural world. In addition
to following migrations, they will observe the local emergence of
spring through studies of changing day length, temperatures and
other spring events. . . .

Journey North will give students the opportunity to interact directly
with scientists and participate in current scientific research on problems not yet solved.

Journey North grew from the initial focus on Arctic wildlife
migrations. The underlying goal was to capture the reasons for
migrations and the change of seasons, helping students understand the relationships between the phenomena. The project
maintained this goal, although continual refinement has occurred
along the way. The underlying premise was that the project content dictates the format—investigations were selected for their
ability to exemplify and capture students' interest in the key concepts related to migration and seasonal change.

The basis in studying natural events as they occur made the
curriculum inherently variable, mandating the use of a flexible,
open-ended approach. Many critical events in the project were
simply not known in advance. This design contrasted with other
projects that determined a curricular model and made the content
fit the model.

Although the project developers believed the Internet offered
potential for interactivity, they only had a peripheral awareness of
the other major telecommunications projects active at the time (e.g.,
NGS Kids Network, FrEdMail/Global SchoolNet, AT&T Learning
Circles). If anything, the content-driven nature of the project was
supported by the circumstances current at the time. The Minnesota-
based Technology and Information Services (TIES) organization had
positioned the state's schools as leaders of technological infrastructure, but TIES needed content-rich projects to make use of the infrastructure already in place. Consequently, an affiliation grew, leading
to Journey North being hosted for a time on the TIES server.

During the first 6 years of the project, modest modifications
strengthened the program content. Species selection was moni-
tored closely in an effort to ensure that the most engaging and
revealing species were tracked. Tracking of some species was
dropped from the program if the migration had not been

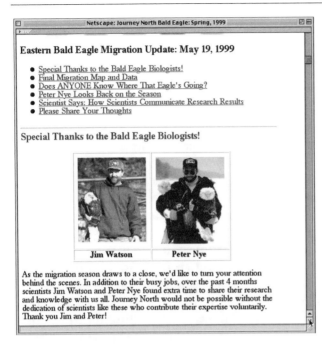

**FIG. 2.4. Journey North provides multiple sources of information to students about the migration of each species.**

www.learner.org/
jnorth/spring1999/
species/eagle/
EUpdate051999.html
[1999, September 9]

sufficiently interesting, if suitable data were not available, or if the data and expertise had not been reliable. Successful activities on species, such as the bald eagle (Fig. 2.4), were enhanced. In 1998, western bald eagles were added to the previously tracked eastern bald eagles, enabling contrasts to be made between the climates and ecosystems on each coast.

For 1998–1999, Journey North experienced a growing enrollment with 4,500 teachers and 200,000 students—up from 1,000 teachers and 60,000 students only 3 years before—and a busy web site with 210,000 hits per month in March and April, 1999.

## Current Challenges

Despite its rapid growth, Journey North faced challenges.

*Long-Term Sustainability.* Journey North was funded through the year 2003, with the expectation of renewal for several years after that. This funding enabled Journey North to be offered to participating classes at no charge. The staff was looking at the potential for a "consortium of agencies committed to developing science projects for students" (Goodman Research Group, 1998) as part of the project's long-term future.

*Expanding the Audience.* Project staff members worked carefully to be aware of the project's audience and to tailor the content accordingly. Although the material was potentially of use to many ages, the interdisciplinary nature of the project lent itself most immediately to self-contained elementary classrooms. This reflected the demographics of users, but Howard and Annenberg/CPB shared the vision of increased involvement among more sophisticated users in middle and high school.

The program was well positioned to attract these older students because much of the data lend themselves to more complex analysis. The teacher's manual did not offer explicit suggestions as to ways in which the investigations can be customized for specific ages, but a resourceful teacher could adapt as needed. For example, the specifics of a given migration (e.g., where a given eagle is and when it left its wintering ground) are appropriate for an upper elementary school student, whereas a middle school student could make year-to-year comparisons or include weather factors into the analysis. In this way, the content knowledge contained in the curriculum could accommodate students at multiple levels, taking into account the developmental stage of an individual class.

Such sophisticated use of the resources would be difficult for a teacher new to inquiry, however, suggesting a need for mentorship in how to select and deploy resources in the most effective manner. The teacher support initiatives discussed next were intended as an avenue toward this goal.

An area that Journey North staff members identified for future development was the inclusion of more resources related to meteorology. This was seen as a significant addition, because weather data were readily available online and the connection among spring, seasonal migration, and weather had the potential to enhance students' understanding of the key science concepts underlying the project.

*User Support.* Teacher training and support also received attention from the Journey North and Annenberg/CPB staffs. The Goodman report indicated that Journey North users often did not feel well supported by the project staff; all four of the other projects that they surveyed reported higher satisfaction with the support they received (Goodman Research Group, 1998). The researchers attributed this finding to the small staff and limited resources available for the task. This perceived lack of effective support did not discourage participation, however. As noted previously, 94% of teachers from the previous year reenrolled for 1997–1998.

Formal teacher training by project staff members was limited to summer workshops in the Minneapolis–St. Paul area and phone support. However, this phone support put quite a strain on the small staff and was not likely to be a viable long-term solution. In the spring of 1998, Journey North added more tutorial and help pages to its web site to assist new users. Plans called for online courses and training videos as part of Annenberg/CPB's effort to incorporate Journey North in support of the goal of improving math and science education on a large scale. The availability of satellite broadcast resources through Annenberg/CPB was a major potential asset in this effort.

Journey North represents a significant departure from the traditional network science model. First, Journey North offered teachers a set of resources from which to draw and support for their use through a teacher's manual, yet it is clearly not a curriculum. Teachers who used it were committed to developing their own curriculum and creating their own schedule. This approach of providing resources rather than a curriculum could be liberating to teachers, but it could be overwhelming to those who needed a model for how to begin. Second, project developers focused on content, with telecommunications technology playing a supplementary role for teachers and students. Any teacher with a web browser (even at home) could participate fully, printing text, data, and maps for student use. This low-technology requirement encouraged participation, but more sophisticated data analysis (such as the vignette described in chap. 6) required more robust software. This was not necessarily a limitation; teachers and students ready for that level of analysis would also be prepared to use higher level software. Third, the data sets—some provided by scientists and some constructed by students—proved capable of sustaining student analysis. By focusing on tangible, specific events (Did the eagle move? Did the tulips bloom at the schools to the south?), students could readily think about the phenomena being studied. Finally, project activities and analysis of the national data sets occurred primarily within each Journey North classroom, rather than among the classrooms.

Each of these features presents a distinct alternative to models described in the first two case studies. By studying each of these three network science curricula—as well as others—we have learned a number of lessons, described in the next chapter, which are important to consider in assessing the current state of network science and envisioning its future.

# 3

# Lessons Learned

**L**ooking across the experiences of multiple network science projects, we see several lessons to be learned. The lessons identified in this chapter are ones that we and our colleagues have found to be central to the success of these network science projects engaging students and teachers in inquiry.

In identifying these lessons, we have drawn on three sources of information. First, we have learned from our experiences working directly with other network science projects over the last 4 years. We consulted with project staff and teachers on technology needs, professional development, and curriculum development, and we observed classrooms. Second, a 2-day invitational conference in November 1997 brought together 33 project leaders, researchers, and experienced network science teachers and provided us with the opportunity to benefit from the rich experiences of our colleagues. We have referred to and quoted from both the preconference statements written by most of the participants and the notes and tape recordings of all the sessions. Third, we have made reference to the findings of the evaluation of the Testbed for Telecollaboration conducted by Goodman Research Group. Their findings are based on detailed interviews with 58 teachers and additional project staff representing five major network science projects.

We begin by looking at lessons about the kind of network science curriculum needed for productive inquiry. Then we look at lessons concerning the technological and human infrastructure needed to support inquiry.

## CURRICULUM TO SUPPORT STUDENT INQUIRY

The primary conclusion of our research is that the Internet is best used to broaden the context of locally grounded inquiry. Effective curriculum uses the Internet as a supportive context that can be employed by curriculum designers and teachers to extend productive inquiries. However, the focus must be local, with the value of the project and the concepts involved comprehensible and meaningful to the student participants at each site. The benchmark against which a network science curriculum might best be judged is the way in which it supports student inquiry—specifically, by the manner in which it helps students develop scientific understanding, skills, and attitudes. There are three critical lessons in this regard:

- Build from interesting questions
- Look locally before globally
- Establish broader perspectives

### Lesson One: Build From Interesting Questions

Good activities and curricula are centered on intrinsically interesting phenomena. However, curriculum writers too often find themselves writing curricula that are constrained by prior decisions about what scientific concepts are to be taught or what technology is to be used. To remedy this situation, curriculum writers need to avoid taking abstract scientific ideas and trying to retrofit them to students' lives. Instead, they should begin with phenomena that students find interesting and then determine which related scientific concepts are within the reach of the students. Only then should developers consider how technologies might enrich or enlarge student explorations.

Nevertheless, it is insufficient to simply say that the topics students investigate should be interesting to them. For a topic to lend itself to productive inquiry, there must also be one or more questions that motivate and focus the work. For example, many students are interested in studying birds at local feeders. Successful implementations of Classroom BirdWatch, however, need to build on that interest to conduct inquiry. Broudy (1988) suggested that when an experience is "trussed up for analysis" (p. 30), a bridge can be made from a student's firsthand experience to the conceptual understandings that help the student make sense of this experience in a broader context.

Bird investigations that focus on questions such as which birds are year-round visitors to the feeders and which are seasonal, or how the local feeder population in one area differs from a feeder population in another area, form the basis of this "trussing up for analysis." By moving from the immediate phenomena of bird watching to broader concepts such as seasonal and regional variations in bird populations and the ecological significance of these variations, students begin to develop their analytic skills. In this way, science moves from being a collection of terms or a series of unconnected observations to a way of seeing patterns, regularities, differences, and consequences.

This focus on going beyond the immediate phenomenon is not meant in any way to demean the value of firsthand experience. On the contrary, it is just this kind of firsthand experience that enables students to become analytic and make connections to scientific concepts. Students who have seen a disturbed colony of ants moving their eggs en masse to safety or who have seen a pill bug drag its prey to hiding form a basis for understanding ecological relationships that they would not develop simply from learning to identify species. Frequent observation and reflection enables students to attain a well-grounded understanding of key ecological concepts such as food chains and prey–predator relationships. Likewise, students who have rolled a variety of objects down ramps at different inclines have the experience that underlies effective inquiry into the laws of motion.

The process of developing the interesting questions that guide an inquiry is challenging, but guiding inquiry with these questions is essential. The choice of what to study and how to focus the investigation through one or more key questions will play a determining role in the success of an inquiry project.

## Lesson Two: Look Locally Before Globally

Although it is quite appropriate to use the power of the Internet to connect students to the global pattern of events, students must not be cut off from local phenomena that can be used to understand events that take place at a distance. The *What's It Like Where You Live?* curriculum (The Evergreen Project, 1996) focuses on biomes or regions defined by the distinctive interaction of climate, plants, and animals. By investigating different biomes, students develop their understanding of key science concepts such as structural and behavioral adaptations and the relationship between form and function.

These concepts are encountered in the context of student investigations of the local climate, plants, and animals. One teacher from the midwest used these investigations as a starting point to help his students develop a useful framework for analyzing other biomes. After conducting extensive fieldwork in a city park, the students had a strong understanding of how the plants and animals characteristic of the temperate deciduous forest adapt to the changing seasons and the local climate conditions.

This framework was then employed as the students used online and video resources to explore other biomes. Virtual deserts and electronic reports from classes in the tundra of the Northwest Territory and the rain forests of Central America took on greater significance in the context of the students' understanding of the temperate deciduous forest, an understanding initially developed through local inquiry. Instead of simply seeing the plants and animals of the other biomes as interesting, the students were able to make a reasonably accurate interpretation of how climate conditions influenced the adaptations in distant places, just as they had seen in the adaptations of local species. Knowing the level of rainfall locally, the students were able to identify water conservation strategies in desert plants as well as water-shedding strategies in the rain forest plants, each strategy being a survival mechanism unique to a particular region.

Note the role of interesting questions in this unit as well. By considering the question "What's it like where you live?" students are guided into a consideration of local conditions and the generation of the framework used for comparisons. Climate, plant, and animal differences among biomes are the key conceptual elements underlying the question, but the broader question of what the area is like provides the glue that holds the inquiry together. Without this integrative question, there is a risk that different concepts being studied may become overly compartmentalized in students' minds. Through investigations of similarities and differences characteristic of each biome, students engage in productive inquiry leading to an understanding of key science concepts relating to biomes and their ability to sustain life.

## Lesson Three: Establish Broader Perspectives

The extension of the local investigations described in the preceding section is one example of a productive local–distant connection that can be established in a network science classroom. The power of the Internet is its ability to promote broader perspectives among students. Whether they are seeing how life forms vary in different parts of the world or coming to appreciate the economic and ecological trade-offs in preserving the monarch butterfly's wintering grounds, students can build on local inquiry to develop perspectives that take into account more complex concepts.

At the Network Science Conference, Susan Wheelwright, a teacher at the Fayerweather School in Cambridge, Massachusetts, shared several examples of how the network component of Journey North had broadened the understanding of her third- and fourth-grade students. The maps stimulated students' interest in geography; a photograph on the Web of a Mexican child driving a truck prompted the students to write him in Spanish to learn how old one had to be to get a Mexican driver's license; the students exuded pure excitement in their responsibility to inform the rest of the Journey North community when Walden Pond melted; the students were fascinated to read an e-mail account of a blizzard in Alaska from other Journey North participants. On this last exchange, Wheelwright remarked that,

> It made a huge impression on my class. They and the Alaskan school were both Americans, both spoke English, but their lives were so incredibly different.

Having acknowledged that the network can be used to place students' observations and experiences in a broader, more global context, we need to add an important caveat: It can only do this if a rich basis of experience has already been established for all students in the classroom. Given this initial experience, the information on the network becomes a context in which they can evaluate their own observations. In Classroom BirdWatch, students can see how their local bird data compare with events happening elsewhere; in One Sky, Many Voices, they can ask how local weather relates to the weather in other parts of the country; and in Journey North, they can see how classroom data fit into the migration pattern over the whole country.

At the same conference, Topher Hagemeier, a staff member of the NGS Kids Network project at TERC, told of the excitement generated among his students several years ago over the inch of snow that fell on their California town. This thrilling news, shared over the Internet, amused students in Minnesota, who wrote back with descriptions of their typical snowfalls. The invitation to students on both ends was to reinterpret their local experience within a broader context. Without the local experiences, the broader context would have held little interest.

Together, these three components—building from interesting questions, looking locally before globally, and using the Internet to establish broader perspectives—have been at the heart of the most successful implementations of network science. They provide valuable lessons as we seek to strengthen the foundation of existing projects and design new ones.

## THE TECHNICAL AND HUMAN INFRASTRUCTURE

The preceding section presented lessons concerning the design of network science curricula that foster local student inquiry augmented by network resources. To realize such a vision requires an appropriate infrastructure. This infrastructure includes technical equipment—hardware, software, and network bandwidth—as well as human support resources in the form of ongoing professional development as teachers grapple with complex technology and new approaches to teaching.

Our experience with a range of network science projects has led us to develop four lessons based on what we have learned about how to construct and maintain this infrastructure:

- Design robust systems
- Prepare teachers for inquiry
- Provide face-to-face communication as well as online experiences for staff development
- Allow time for learning and change

## Lesson Four: Design Robust Systems

In the ideal world, network science projects are implemented in a classroom and school in which the technological infrastructure is sufficient to complete the tasks. The reality often falls short of the ideal, however, and many pioneering teachers have worked valiantly to carry out projects lacking the computers and Internet connections needed for effective implementation. Often they have plunged into projects only to find that promised hardware and network installations are behind schedule in their district. Although it is certainly true that computers are becoming more prevalent in schools, it is still a rare classroom that has all the hardware and software needed for ideal implementation. Even when it does, it still is not immune from network outages and repair problems.

Consequently, project developers need to design systems that are robust in the following dimensions:

- They can be carried out in classrooms utilizing widely varying levels of technology and in schools with a variety of local infrastructures;
- they are not crippled by local infrastructure problems; and
- they are not crippled by the failures of other schools on the network to participate.

An example of a robust design is one used by One Sky, Many Voices. This project distributes a CD-ROM that contains most of the resources needed to carry out the project. This reduces the vulnerability associated with getting and staying online and with sluggish data transfers. It also reduces the number of Internet connections required in a classroom. A single connection can be dedicated to retrieving information that involves frequent updating, such as the path of an ongoing storm, whereas the other computers require only CD-ROM drives from which students can access simulations, tutorials, and archives. Schools with ample connections can have students interact with the network resources more directly, whereas schools with a limited number of connections can also participate effectively.

The revised web-based NGS Kids Network is another example of robust design. The units begin as personal explorations ("my data") and evolve into explorations with broader contexts ("our classroom data" and "the network data"). One advantage of this strategy is that conducting the data-rich units no longer depends on the timely exchange of information over the network. Even if the network connections fail, or if a large percentage of classes do not contribute data, students can still make sense of their local data and archival data. These features add strength to the investigations that classes pursue because student inquiry is enhanced by—but not dependent on—network data.

Joel Halvorson, a staff member of Journey North, advises teachers to avoid Internet-based projects, i.e., projects that are overly bound to the Internet in the same way that traditional instruction is bound to the blackboard. He noted at the conference that, "It's important that teachers be able to engage kids if they are given nothing but a bare room with four walls." Speaking to fellow project developers, he warned that, "If a project does not have the ability to stand on its own without the technology, then the technology is not going to be able to deliver anything." It is the curriculum that must be robust, not the technology.

## Lesson Five: Prepare Teachers for Inquiry

To implement network science projects effectively, teachers need support in using new teaching approaches and curriculum units, as well as new computer tools and network connections. Consequently, it is not surprising that teachers never fully implement network science projects in their initial years. Teachers need time and support to develop a comfort level with each of these features. Because of time constraints and funding priorities faced by many projects, professional development currently does not receive the level of support needed for effective implementation of network science.

Given these limitations, staff development initiatives need to be prioritized. Three areas that project staff members can deal with directly deserve the highest priority: creating a vision of an inquiry-oriented curriculum, extending teachers' understanding of relevant science content, and designing effective uses of data to support investigations. Each of these needs attention as part of the project development and implementation process, and each has consistently posed challenges to implementation efforts.

*Creating a Vision of an Inquiry-Oriented Curriculum.* Although we initially took for granted that network science projects adequately model for teachers how to lead inquiry-oriented class-rooms, we found that most teachers need far more help envision-ing how such a classroom can function. With this support, teachers can overcome the impression that inquiry is "just too hard to implement" in practice.

A first step toward such a vision is for teachers to experience inquiry themselves. Many teachers have experienced in their own science education an approach to science that did not value inquiry. Consequently, a majority of network science project participants have little experience generating questions, collecting data, and debating alternative explanations. This lack of experience with vital elements of inquiry, coupled with the transmission model of peda-gogy that is currently so prevalent in practice, obscures teachers' views of how their own teaching can be transformed. Thus, the first step in creating an inquiry-rich vision among teachers is for them to participate in their own investigations.

As teachers gain experience conducting their own inquiries, they begin to see the value of having students conduct inquiries. Many, however, have a difficult time linking their own experiences with issues of pedagogy and classroom management. To bridge this gap, staff development efforts need to present models to par-ticipants. Workshop sessions led by master teachers experienced in classroom applications of network science are invaluable. The credibility of a teacher who has implemented inquiry-oriented cur-riculum in a real classroom can make a major contribution to teachers being able to see how they might implement network sci-ence. Also, a number of videos are available for staff development. These show inquiry classes in action and highlight pedagogic techniques (National Gardening Association, 1991; Rosebery & Warren, 1996).

*Extending Content Knowledge.* As with any inquiry-oriented curriculum, network science projects rely on teachers' under-standing of the science content to support the investigations tak-ing place. The goal of augmenting content knowledge is not to help the teacher become a walking encyclopedia on the subject, but to provide the intellectual context needed for them to make the many small but critical decisions required as the project unfolds. Knowledge helps teachers guide students toward productive paths of inquiry, select resources to have available in class, and conduct productive discussions.

The challenge that many network science projects encounter is how to provide the level of support needed to ensure that teachers are comfortable with the concepts underlying the project activities (such as migration routes or energy conservation measures). To that end, individual projects have implemented a number of strategies.

Some network science programs have expanded sections of the teacher's guide or the web site to identify key ideas. For example, NGS Kids Network teacher's guides include a "Core Ideas" section for each of the lessons. Also, by previewing the selected web sites associated with each lesson, teachers can deepen their understanding of the material. The Journey North manual and web site provide supplementary background material that can be used by students and teachers to augment their understanding of specific animals or signs of spring. Links to other sites (such as the Save the Manatee Foundation) provide supplementary content resources.

Onsite staff development is an enormous logistic challenge especially for nationally dispersed projects. Several projects have made significant efforts in this regard. NGS Kids Network employs a cadre of workshop instructors who present training nationally. EnergyNet has conducted summer training sessions involving teachers from across Illinois. Journey North has conducted training workshops near its home in the Minneapolis–St. Paul area.

Cornell Lab of Ornithology received a 3-year grant to support teachers in their use of the Classroom BirdWatch curriculum. This project, the Schoolyard Ornithology Resource Project (SORP), seeks to develop and disseminate a staff development model for enhancing teachers' content knowledge—in this case, bird ecology.

Ideally, a workshop will prepare teachers intellectually and psychologically to lead their classes in inquiry. Each of these examples aims to equip the teachers with the background needed to provide such leadership. Although none provides a replacement for a teacher's experience and general background knowledge, such targeting of information can make a difference in how confidently a teacher supports student inquiry.

*Supporting Effective Data Use.* As students and teachers engage in an inquiry-based network science program, they will collect a range of data. Across all projects, a clear need for support around data issues is evident. As the Goodman Research Group (1998) evaluation report pointed out, 84% of participating teachers said they needed help with data issues. "Many of them indicated they...have trouble with data analysis on their own, let alone sharing data using the Internet" (p. 70). The result is that examples of substantive discussion and analysis of the data are virtually nonexistent in our research and in the work conducted by others (e.g., Karlan, Huberman, & Middlebrooks, 1997).

Students and teachers need to develop basic data analysis skills to make sense of data that are often complex and almost never as "clean" as the data sets provided in prefabricated worksheets. These skills include the following as a basic tool kit of data literacy:

- choosing and measuring relevant variables;
- representing data effectively in charts, graphs, and maps;
- developing and communicating findings effectively; and
- using data sets to generate new perspectives and inquiries.

Classroom data use is the most difficult of the professional development needs. The request for support with data use is not limited to teachers. The Goodman Research Group (1998) reported that "both teachers and project staff requested assistance [in] developing approaches to help teachers use data" (p. 75). There is a clear need for a major initiative on this subject—one larger than any individual curriculum can initiate. Our recommendations on this subject are detailed in chapter 5.

## Lesson Six: Online Staff Development Cannot Replace Face-to-Face Communication

Most network science projects have attempted to develop online communities for teacher support, with varying degrees of teacher participation. The great hope attached to these online communities is that they will provide a dynamic forum in which project members reflect deeply on their experiences and exchange perspectives relating to the project.

At the conference, this issue was discussed at length. Deborah Muscella, director of LabNet, suggested that projects use online communities to "leverage teacher expertise so that teachers come to view themselves as experts and begin providing that expertise to other teachers." In this way, a true virtual community would be realized. In the experience of EnergyNet Director Carol Timms, online community support "doesn't work unless we've built first the one-[to]-one relationship." Charlie Hutchison, a researcher on Testbed for Telecollaboration, elaborated on this idea by making a distinction between strong and weak communities. He argued that, in a weak community, links enabled by the network may not be sufficient to support learning and development. Ironically, it is just such a strong local support base that was found to correlate with low participation in online communities, with teachers reporting that their needs for professional dialogue were being met locally (McMahon, 1996).

Ray Rose, a project director at the Concord Consortium, countered that he believed online communities could be developed in the absence of this face-to-face interaction. "The secret," Rose said in reference to his experiences with Virtual High School classes, "is spending some time at the beginning on community building. The community must come first, and then you can move on to the other work." This model is unproved as a guide for professional development, however, because the current approach to professional development in the Virtual High School includes regular face-to-face meetings.

As desirable as these teacher communities seem, they are rarely seen in practice—either with network science projects or elsewhere. In her report on the Mathematics Learning Forum, an online course designed to support a virtual community of math teachers with regular exchanges of ideas and perspectives, McMahon (1996) stated that fewer than half of the participants averaged contributing one message a week. By the end of the 8-week course, only 15% of the original participants were still involved. The substance of the online discussion consisted in large part of social discussions and opportunities to "gather tips and strategies" (p. 148), instead of debate and collaborative discussion of challenging professional issues.

Experience to date shows that online communities are not an effective replacement for face-to-face professional dialogue, although individual vignettes suggest that there are possibilities in the medium yet to be uncovered. Further research and development on this subject may lead to ways of tapping the currently dormant promise of online professional communities.

## Lesson Seven: Allow Time for Learning and Change

If the vision of learning and instruction informing network science projects is to be realized, fundamental shifts are required in pedagogical thinking and institutional cultures. Improvements in technology tools and infrastructures will not solve the need for such fundamental shifts. Significant change, at every level, requires adequate support, the financial resources needed to deliver new programs, and time. In its conclusion, the Goodman Research Group (1998) characterized network science as a "developmental practice" (p. 71), pointing out that teachers need time and support to become familiar and comfortable with the multiple layers of the projects.

In reflecting on his work in teacher training programs, Jimmy Karlan, author of a research study about NGS Kids Network and current director of the Environmental Studies Teacher Certification Program at Antioch New England Graduate School, described for conference participants his experiences working with teachers to develop their pedagogical philosophy. He pointed to the need to overcome the many psychological barriers to teaching through inquiry, including fear of losing control and fears of feeling inadequate to manage an inquiry that may go in unpredictable directions. While trying to figure out what he can do differently, he reminded his colleagues that results are not always immediately evident: "I can plant a seed." Candace Julyan of the Arnold Arboretum in Boston echoed the same belief:

> Change takes a long time. You could go into a lot of classrooms and not see anything remotely close to what you'd want to see in an inquiry classroom. But I think if you kept going back every year, you'd see a shift.

It is easy to forget the difficulties faced by teachers with no prior exposure to computers and without local support when they begin to use technology at the same time they are experimenting with innovative curriculum. Teacher Susan Wheelwright was already doing similar ecology investigations when she learned about Journey North from a parent of one of her students. Despite her comfort with the project's pedagogy and content, she gave herself 3 years to fully incorporate the project's technology components. "When I learned that first year that I could be doing all [of] this on the Web, I said, 'No way, I couldn't take that all in. I'll just do it through e-mail,' which was also new to me." The second year, she accessed the Web through the library computer, where she could count on the support of nearby staff. It was only in the third year that she began using the Internet connection in her classroom.

Just as teachers need time to develop their skills in leading an inquiry-oriented class, students also need multiple experiences with this type of curriculum to learn the set of expectations that accompany this method. For students used to more didactic pedagogy, inquiry can be unsettling. Bob Coulter, a former third-grade teacher who made extensive use of network science projects in a traditional school setting, reported the initial confusion of his students. When moving into a new area of inquiry, he gave them the time they needed "to just mess around" in a manner similar to that advocated by Hawkins (1974) years ago. Many of Coulter's students were initially uneasy with this open-ended approach and tried to guess what they should be thinking. "I don't know what you want me to be interested in," one of his third-grade students complained during the early part of a project.

Significant and lasting change takes time. Curriculum designers and school personnel need to account for this by providing means to structure implementation over a period of years and by tempering expectations of immediate, measurable gains.

Part I of this volume looked at the history and state of the art in network science. From the early excitement generated a decade ago to the more tempered—but no less hopeful—approaches taken today, we recounted and analyzed the best efforts to make use of networking technologies to improve students' science learning.

As we reflect on this decade of experience, two teaching strategies stand out as being particularly problematic. Sustaining reflective discourse in the classroom and engaging in productive data analysis have both proved to be inordinately difficult goals to achieve.

These two strategies must be reexamined and redesigned for the goals of network science to be realized. To that end, we offer extended analyses of these two strategies in Part II, in hopes of contributing to the professional dialogue that needs to take place around classroom discourse and data analysis.

Part II

# Looking Deeply

# Promoting Reflective Discourse

S tudents engaged in discussions—raising questions, testing ideas, challenging each other's assertions—is at the heart of inquiry learning. Such discussions enable students to go beyond hands-on activities to interpret and reflect on their experiences and develop new ways of thinking.

Reflecting their understanding of inquiry learning, the originators of network science aimed to have students in distant classrooms use the network to discuss science with one another like collaborating scientists. This chapter focuses on the empirical question of whether such substantive discussions occur over the network among students. Our research indicates that online discussions in network science curricula are typically social in nature and not related to the substance of the science being studied.

Why aren't more substantive discussions occurring online? To begin to answer this question, we look at the transcript of a discussion in a high school science classroom and point to the complex role of the teacher in shaping these discussions and in establishing the classroom culture to support them. If similar discussions are to occur over the network, participants would need to establish a similar culture that supported these discussions—a problematic proposition in an online context.

Although little research is currently available, we hypothesize that the Internet may be used to support substantive, reflective exchanges among students who have learned to carry on similar conversations in the science classroom, but that the Internet is an unlikely place for students to learn how to engage in such discussions.

## CLASSROOM COLLABORATIONS: THE VISION

Networked communications between distant classrooms is meant to provide the motivation and basis for substantive scientific discussions. The sharing of data around a common question sets the stage for such discussions, giving students a common base of observations that together they try to understand and explain. The vision has been that the network, together with the common objectives, would allow students to undertake authentic, collaborative science. In their role as colleagues and collaborators, students might critique or challenge claims made by other students, ask that terms and claims be clarified, and inquire about sources and meaning of data—all for the purpose of better understanding what other students are saying. These mutual obligations would stimulate and fertilize thinking. In working to make themselves understandable, students would be driven to deeper understandings of their data and the scientific phenomena they are investigating.

This vision stands in contrast to class discussions that typically occur in U.S. schools. Mehan (1979) and others have described these discussions as following the IRE pattern. The teacher *Initiates* interaction with a question ("What is gravity?"), a student gives a simple *Response* ("It's the earth pulling on us"), and the teacher *Evaluates* the response ("That's correct"). This evaluation tends to be brief and is typically followed by the next question ("Does gravity involve only the earth pulling?"), setting up the next stage of IRE. The discussion proceeds on the assumption that teachers know the answers to questions they pose. When combined with the characteristic 1-second wait time for students to begin to answer (Rowe, 1983), the IRE pattern says to students, "You either know the answer to a question or you don't." Generating and weighing alternative answers, working through multistep solutions, examining assumptions, and reflecting on methods—all the various skills we associate with critical and reflective thinking—are left by the wayside in the hope of first developing a store of knowledge. As long ago as 1929, Whitehead referred to such knowledge as *inert* because it cannot be applied to appropriate situations or used to solve practical problems.

Early advocates of network science hoped that the use of the network would help classrooms break this pattern by providing both authentic questions for students' investigations (ones for which the teachers did not know the answers) and real audiences for students' thinking and work. The belief that real audiences could change the nature of communication in the classroom is a compelling one. Consider the students' typical audience. For example, a student writing a report on the water cycle is most likely writing for the teacher, who presumably already knows more than the student does about the topic. The teacher reads the report not to learn about the water cycle, but to formulate a judgment about student performance and perhaps to offer constructive feedback. Through writing the report and conducting the required background research, a student learns more about the water cycle. However, once written, the report is simply an object for evaluation, not a tool for communication. The student pretends to be an expert in writing the report, whereas the teacher pretends to be a somewhat naive audience while reading it. The teacher reverts to the role of expert in giving feedback to the student, and the student reverts to the role of novice in accepting that feedback.

Audiences envisioned in network science are real because they do not know beforehand what other students are trying to say, and they are not there to render an evaluative judgment. Neither the students nor the audience pretend to know any more or less than they do while writing or reading a communication. The audience is neither a passive consumer of nor a cheering section for the work of the student. Under such conditions, it is certainly reasonable that students might regard questions they investigate more seriously and critically.

## CLASSROOM COLLABORATIONS: THE REALITY

The preceding rationale for how network science would set the stage for substantive discussions seems reasonable. Unfortunately, we still see few instances of these sorts of dialogue occurring among network science classrooms. Most of the messages posted in the public discussion spaces are of the hello variety—social chatter about the school, student interests and characteristics, and requests for factual information (e.g., "Does anybody know ...?"). Table 4.1 categorizes 89 messages exchanged among classrooms on the Global Lab bulletin board during the first half of the 1997–1998 school year.[9] These messages do not include communications that served as announcements from project staff (24) or exchanges among teachers about pedagogy (35, most of which were teaching tips).

TABLE 4.1

TYPES OF MESSAGES ON THE GLOBAL LAB BULLETIN BOARD

| Message Form | Message Content | | |
| | About Us | About Science | Total |
| --- | --- | --- | --- |
| Sharing | 67 | 14 | 81 |
| Asking | 1 | 6 | 7 |
| Responding | 1 | 0 | 1 |

The majority of messages consist of students sharing information about themselves and their schools ("About Us"). Six messages pose questions to others about the topic under investigation, but not one message is responded to.

A couple of caveats are in order. First, although they may seem unproductive, chatty exchanges are an important part of the social fabric that supports collaborative efforts. They may connect students to a larger world, establish rapport and trust, and provide context for evaluating substantive data from collaborating sites. For example, a comment such as "What a day! Spring weather has finally arrived" may help another class understand a reported change in conditions at the partner school's local study site.

Second, we expect that the more substantive exchanges would take place point to point over e-mail rather than in public forums. We have not had access to these private e-mail communications among classrooms. If substantive exchanges were occurring over e-mail, however, we would expect to hear about them from the project staff, who are typically on the lookout for interesting classroom collaborations. Our repeated inquiries to project staff and teachers soliciting their help to identify such exchanges have yielded little.

We also have some data from Classroom BirdWatch, a science curriculum that encourages middle school classes to form research partnerships and communicate with one another on a regular basis. The following comments are the responses of teachers to a questionnaire distributed at the end of the first year.[10] These suggest that the private communications between research partners often follow the same pattern seen in public spaces. In general, the comments center on the students rather than the science.

> I think they [the students] would like to be more personal. Most of the info is surface data about our project. None has been very specific.

> They want to tell their partner about their class, school, themselves and what they were doing in the project.

Several Classroom BirdWatch teachers reported that when they tried to initiate dialogue about the science, their queries went unanswered:

> We have updated our weather and observations but have not heard back from our partners.

> We also talked about the fact that the mourning doves seem to prefer the seeds on the ground rather than the platform of our feeder. We asked if our research partners had noticed the same things or if they thought the coloration of the mourning dove had anything to do with them preferring the ground to the platform. [We've heard nothing yet, but] I will keep pushing for ongoing communication.

The potential value of using the network as a source for getting their own questions answered is evident to these teachers and their classes. However, the learning opportunities in responding to someone else's questions are apparently more subtle. Seeing these opportunities requires, among other things, understanding how reflective discourse promotes learning—an issue we explore in the following section.

## REFLECTIVE DISCOURSE

By *reflective discourse* we mean a conversation in which students do one or more of the following:

- Request clarification of terms or processes. *How did you measure acidity?*
- Ask questions about the meaning or accuracy of data. *Did you guys really get a soil pH of 2?*

- Question warrants. *What were your reasons for concluding that the trees around your school account for the acidic soil?*

The following explores the nature of reflective discourse and how a classroom teacher can support this discourse. As part of this analysis, we view classroom discourse from two different perspectives of learning: constructivist and sociocultural.

## Mentored Reflective Discourse

van Zee and Minstrell (1997a) referred to *reflective discourse* as a discussion in which "students express their own thoughts in comments and questions rather than recite textbook answers." (p. 212) This includes discussions in which

> the teacher and individual students engage in extended series of questioning exchanges that help students articulate their beliefs and conceptions; and student/student exchanges [which] involve one student trying to understand the thinking of another (p. 212).

Varelas (1996) described similar classroom discourse by the underlying pedagogical objectives of the teacher:

> Discourse allows students to express their own thinking, negotiate ideas and understandings with fellow students and their teacher, and develop them further. During discourse, students' own ways of thinking and knowing are revealed, allowing the teacher to identify students' understandings, validate them as ways of reasoning about the subject matter, and also help the students develop these understandings further. (p. 233)

We believe that *reflective discourse*, as defined earlier, is both educationally important and difficult to sustain among students; it requires the active involvement of a teacher who understands the role of such discourse and who has developed classroom practices that value and support the discussion. We refer to such discussion when orchestrated by the teacher as *mentored reflective discourse*. The purpose of this discourse is to stimulate student learning through reflective thinking and discussion.

Table 4.2 describes in general terms some of the teacher behaviors that characterize mentored reflective discourse along with some of the educational objectives the teacher has in mind. These behaviors and objectives reflect the key role of the teacher

TABLE 4.2

BEHAVIOR AND OBJECTIVES OF REflECTIVE DISCOURSE

| Teacher Behavior | Teacher Objective |
|---|---|
| Encourage students to formulate and express their own theories. | Students learn to offer possible explanations rather than recite correct answers. Teacher gains insights into student thinking. |
| Encourage students to ask one another for clarifications and elaborations. | Students come to assume responsibility for understanding one another. Students clarify their thinking. |
| Give nonevaluative responses. | Students come to see themselves as having authority to judge answers. |
| Redirect questions to other students. | Students come to see themselves as capable of answering many of their own questions. |
| Engage students in making predictions from their theories. | Students learn to evaluate theories by testing predictions. |
| Allow sufficient wait times. | Students come to value thoughtful comments that may require time to formulate. |

in mentored reflective discourse. Beyond guiding the discussion into fruitful areas, the teacher shapes classroom conversations by modeling and reinforcing values and establishing agreements and conventions. We refer to these values, agreements, and conventions as *classroom norms*.

## An Example of Classroom Discourse

Here we examine in some detail an example of mentored reflective discourse from van Zee and Minstrell (1997a). Our purpose is to give substance to the preceding discussion, especially the importance of classroom norms and the key role teachers play in guiding student discussions.

The discussion took place in Jim Minstrell's high school physics class in Mercer Island High School, Washington. Minstrell posed the question of whether an object that weighed 10 pounds on a spring scale would weigh any more or less if weighed in a vacuum. After he was sure the students understood the situation, Minstrell asked that students individually generate a prediction and justification for that prediction based on their current understandings.

T:  I don't expect you to have the answers at this point but you've lived in a world that has [been influenced by gravity] for some 16 to 19 years already and so you really do have some understanding of the nature of gravity and its effects.

Here Minstrell encouraged students to draw on what they knew. He attempted to put them at ease about describing their predictions and justifications—he did not expect them at this point to hold scientifically accurate ideas about gravity. The next discussion took place after students had individually written explanations for their answers.

T:  All right. Now in walking around [the room], I saw several different answers. . . .

And as I look at the answers there, they ranged from up around 15 to 20, to, ah, down around 12, 11, a little more than 10; some people said it'd be just 10, same as what it weighted before; ah, others said a little less than 10, 9 something like that, and, ah, other folks said, about zero, or a tiny bit more than zero, or something like that.

Now in this case, let's hold off attacks on other answers yet and let's, first of all, defend one or another of those answers. Okay?

[S1]?

S1:  Uh, I put zero, because, um, I thought (laughs) that there's no air; it's kind of like the moon where those astronauts float around and they have no—they have no, ah, weight; so I put zero [unintelligible].

T:  Okay. It's like being on the moon and on the moon, there's no weight and so they sort of bound around. No weight; there's no air there. Okay?

Minstrell requested that students not yet critique one another's ideas. Instead, he modeled what he wanted them to do—strive to understand what a particular student was saying. Accordingly, he offered a paraphrase of S1's explanation. In his restatement, he gave no indication that he either agreed or disagreed with the student's thesis. Among other things, this neutrality creates a safe atmosphere for the expression of student ideas.

Several other students offered predictions and rationales. In each case, Minstrell tried to summarize their rationales to check his understanding of what they had said. He then invited students to challenge one another's thinking.

T:　All right. Now, ah, you might start looking at, if you, if you've got ways of answering somebody else's argument, without beating up on them here and drawing blood or something [that'll] be OK too; if you've got some argument that counters one of the other arguments [S14]?

S14:　About what [S2] said about the air pressure pushing up on it?

T:　Uh huh.

S14:　I don't think that'd be true because air doesn't push up, just because gravity pushes down . . . so there's no air that's helping it to stay up really.

T:　So there's no air helping it stay up?

S14:　Yeah. But there is air there.

T:　But there is air around. So what would you argue for?

S14:　[Like [S10] said] (gestures to student sitting behind him) A little bit less than ten.

T:　It's a little bit less than ten.

S14:　Yeah (nods head).

T:　Okay.

Here again, Minstrell remained neutral on the particulars of the criticism offered by S14, trying only to understand the objection to S2's reasoning. When several students began questioning one another, Minstrell withdrew momentarily from the discussion.

S15:　[unintelligible] What were you saying now?

S14:　Okay. There's air pressure pushing down on it.

S15:　Right. Wait, there's air pressure pushing down on it.

S14:   [Okay. There's nothing pushing up. Gravity pulls the air down.]

S15:   [S14], in water, if you had something in that, it would be lighter. Correct?

S16:   But we're not talking about water.

S15:   Nevertheless, um, air is also denser than no air, as water is denser than air, you see? Do you understand the relation there?

S14:   Yeah. Okay.

S12:   What I was thinking about water was that if it's pressing down, if you're far enough under the water, the water pressure would crush you.

S15:   Exactly, if you go high enough up in the atmosphere, the pressure would be way less than the pressure down here, as in water as you go further down.

T:     Okay, all right. It sounds like there's some arguments then, some pretty good arguments here [from] pretty well all across the spectrum.

It is worth noting that several of the behaviors Minstrell had just been modeling appeared in this exchange among the students. First, students questioned each other about the reasonableness of their underlying models. S15 began by asking S14 to clarify a claim that had been made. Although S15 began to offer a counterargument, he or she remained respectful and even stopped to ask whether the argument offered made sense to S14 ("Do you understand the relation there?"). Minstrell finally interrupted the discussion, perhaps sensing that the students were not going to progress much further. He concluded, however, by reminding students that the purpose of the discussion had been to raise and understand a variety of arguments rather than arrive at an agreed-on view.

What was absent from the discussion is also notable. The students were not asking Minstrell to reveal the correct answer, nor did they seem frustrated by the presentation and discussion of multiple points of view. On the contrary, judging from the transcript, they seemed to enjoy the opportunity to offer and argue their respective positions.

Minstrell then led a discussion about how to design an experiment to determine what effect air has on the weight of an object.

They agreed that they would place an object in a bell jar and then weigh them together. They would do the weighing before, and then after, removing all the air from the bell jar. Before conducting the experiment, he asked students to show, by raise of hands, whether the scale reading would increase, decrease, or stay about the same when the air was removed. Then he invited some of the students to observe the reading of the scale as the air was removed from the bell jar. After they had agreed that there was no noticeable change in the weight when the air was removed, he asked them to summarize the experiment.

T:  What does that tell us about the main effect then of gravity and air pressure? (3-second pause)

S:  It's not gravity. (4-second pause)[11]

T:  They're apparently different, different sorts of things? Gravity and air pressure are not the same?

Minstrell's main objective in this session was to help students differentiate gravity from air pressure—two constructs that many conflate (e.g., S1). Therefore, he chose to ignore, for the time being, the small buoyancy effect due to air that S15 had articulated rather well.

## Comparing Types of Discussions

This classroom episode stands in contrast to the IRE pattern described earlier. Although parts of the discussion among Minstrell and his students might seem to have followed the IRE structure, they tended to end not with evaluations but with neutral responses, such as "Okay."[12] Furthermore, many common features of discussions in Minstrell's classroom never occur in IRE exchanges. In a "reflective toss" (van Zee & Minstrell, 1997b), Minstrell takes a question or idea from one student and throws it back to that student or other students for discussion:

S14:  Yeah. But there is air there.

T:  But there is air around. So what would you argue for?

Another type of class discussion we have observed involves the teacher encouraging students to share solution strategies or ideas. "Can anyone tell us what gravity is?" (Mary gives her explanation.) "Thank you, Mary. Someone else?" (Bill gives his explanation.)

"Thank you, Bill." This type of discussion could be a part of a mentored reflective discourse if the teacher and students elaborate on or critique those ideas. For example, the teacher could then encourage the students to consider the validity of various explanations or devise means of testing them. Teachers just beginning to incorporate reflective discussions in their classroom may often not know where to go with a discussion. As a result, the discussion may not progress beyond the simple sharing of viewpoints.

An observer of a class engaged in mentored reflective discourse may misconstrue the purpose of the discussion as allowing students to learn for themselves without teacher guidance. As Schoenfeld, Minstrell, and van Zee (1996) pointed out, however, what might appear to an outsider to be an uncharted, spontaneous discussion is, in fact, a highly structured and fairly predictable set of discussions and activities from the teacher's perspective.

> Minstrell [is] on very familiar ground a large part of the time [during these discussions], knowing what students are likely to produce and having access to reflective tosses to keep the conversation going. (p. 8)

Thus, mentored reflective discourse is not undertaken by a teacher with the assumption that students will discover for themselves the principles of science, but rather with relatively clear images of students' current understandings, where they can be after some instruction, and the steps or transitions they need to go through to get there. Before the discussion begins, the teacher has in mind a hypothetical learning trajectory (Simon, 1995) that specifies how students' conceptions can develop to resemble normative scientific conceptions.

It is worth reviewing briefly the student-as-scientist perspective described in chapter 1 as being part of the founding vision of network science. Although we are ardent advocates of student discourse, we question the value of viewing conversations among students in a science classroom as analogous to scientific discourse. Simply put, it is not sufficient to provide students with the means to communicate with one another or even with a reason to communicate. Unlike the discourse of scientists, student discourse requires the skillful and active participation of a teacher to establish the norms that underlie scientific discourse and make it different from everyday conversation.

## The Role of Reflective Discourse in Learning

We digress from the earlier focus on class discussions to consider different perspectives on learning. Our purpose is to use these perspectives to examine further how mentored reflective discourse supports student learning and why the role of the teacher is critical in establishing the classroom norms for such discourse.

The objectives that guide Minstrell's pedagogical choices have been informed by perspectives on learning that have become increasingly influential during the last 15 years, especially in mathematics and science education. One of these perspectives, constructivism, highlights the central role that students' current knowledge plays in what they perceive and learn in new situations. The other, a sociocultural view, gives priority to social aspects of learning and shows how shared goals, established norms, and other social patterns determine what counts as knowledge.

## A Constructivist's View

According to von Glasersfeld (1984), as knowers we do not have direct access to the external world. Rather, we use what we already know to select and interpret what we perceive. From this perspective, perception and learning are not passive acts of taking in information, but rather active, constructive processes by which we select, organize, and impose meaning on incoming stimuli. We have the impression that we perceive an orderly, organized world. However, all we really know is that we have managed to create order in our own minds.

Constructivist views, many less radical than von Glaserfield, inspired a flood of studies beginning in the late 1970s that examined the informal beliefs students brought to the study of various mathematics and science topics (for reviews, see Driver & Erickson, 1983; Confrey, 1990). Many of these studies demonstrated that traditional instruction typically failed to alter student beliefs. This research was used to argue for new methods of instruction and, in particular, for putting less emphasis on memorization and the teaching of formalisms and more on students' underlying conceptual understanding.[13] Of particular importance is the role of failure in setting the stage for learning.

According to most constructivists, when we face a new situation, we initially apply what we already know to understand it and achieve the desired goal. Piaget referred to this process as *assimilation*. Sometimes, however, we are not able to apply existing knowledge successfully. This lack of success sets the stage for *accommodation*, modifying our current understanding to better fit the new situation. Thus, in this perspective, it is the failure to apply existing knowledge to achieve desired objectives that drives learning.

General aspects of Minstrell's mentored classroom dialogue are motivated by this constructivist view of learning. In particular, the entire discussion is structured around a theorize-predict-test-evaluate cycle in which students first articulate their current understanding of a situation. On the basis of these theories, students make predictions about the outcome of an experiment. The experiment is then conducted, setting the stage for some of the students to reconsider their theories, or conceptual models, as their predictions are not confirmed.

> In this approach teachers first determine what ideas students have on a scientific topic before they have received instruction. The teacher then uses these ideas to create impasses in student reasoning, and assists students as they learn new material by resolving these impasses. (Hunt & Minstrell, 1995)

This basic view of learning is evident in the features of the preceding classroom dialogues, the most prominent being the importance of eliciting student theories. In giving a significant role to prior knowledge in students' thinking, a constructivist approach typically involves engaging students in an activity by encouraging them to draw on what they already know, as Minstrell did. The difficulties they eventually encounter provide opportunities for them to construct new understandings. Missteps and mistakes are viewed as an essential part of learning. The overriding message to students is that their job is to understand.

Because the responsibility for learning is ultimately that of the individual, the key instructional unit in the constructivist classroom is the student. From this perspective, the teacher's role is somewhat vague, but is often portrayed as that of a personal coach. Each individual comes to a particular activity with a different set of prior beliefs. The teacher can assist by gaining insight into each student's perspective and using this insight to monitor progress and tailor instruction.

From this point of view, the class discussions that Minstrell orchestrates serve two important pedagogical functions. First, they give Minstrell insight into how individual students are thinking. Second, given that students publicly commit to certain predictions and claims, the discussions set the stage for *disequilibration*, as students' expectations and prior beliefs conflict with the views of others.

## A Sociocultural View

In our portrayal, constructivist pedagogy is built on the need for individual students to struggle to integrate or make sense of some new experience that does not fit with existing knowledge. Knowledge is construed as belonging to an individual—as residing in a person's head. In a variety of sociocultural views on knowledge and learning, many inspired by the work of Vygotsky, sense making is not seen as happening independently, but as being coordinated among members of a group and intimately tied to the social practices in which they jointly engage. For some writers who have developed sociocultural views, the individual appears to reflect more the social collective than an autonomous existence.

This distinction—individual vs. sociocultural perspectives—has influenced the thinking of educators. For example, Scardamalia and Bereiter (1996) contrasted "students as individuals engaged in the processes of scientific inquiry" with "the class as a collective engaged in the processes of a scientific community" (p. 253). The former description, characteristic of early inquiry curricula, suggests a constructivist perspective; the latter, a sociocultural perspective.

After briefly describing one sociocultural perspective, we look again at Minstrell's class discussions to see how they may facilitate learning in a way not accounted for within a purely constructivist view. We also identify classroom norms needed to initiate and sustain such discussions. We maintain that if similar discussions are to occur over the network, the participants would have to establish a comparable set of norms—a problematic proposition in an online context.

Lave and Wenger (1991) offered an interesting sociocultural analysis of apprenticeship systems. According to them, all learning is situated within communities, and knowledge is developed in concert with the social-physical practices of the community. Learning is seen as an integral and inseparable aspect of the social practices. It is not the achievement of one person struggling alone to understand, but an accomplishment distributed among coparticipants striving for common goals.[14] Lave and Wenger developed the notion of *legitimate peripheral participation* to describe the structural practices that allow novices to participate from the beginning in the activities of the specialized community, supported by experts who structure the tasks, model good practice, provide needed support, and gradually fade these supports. In this way, novices gain "access to sources for understanding through growing involvement" (p. 37).

This sociocultural perspective offers another way to interpret what happens in Minstrell's classroom. Rather than seeing his objective simply as encouraging individual students to articulate and then perhaps revise their conceptual understandings, we see him trying to establish a particular classroom culture—one that resembles a scientific community. He uses the occasion of working on the weight problem to initiate students into a scientist-like style of thinking and discourse. He orchestrates the activity, providing structure that allows students to participate as best they can, and then fades this support to allow students to carry on discussions in which they are questioning one another and seeking to understand the situation by themselves.

Such discussions are often described as a negotiation among students and their teachers about the meaning of a situation, about what the goals should be, and about how those goals can be achieved. The social sphere in which this negotiation takes places has been characterized as a *construction zone* (Newman, Griffin, & Cole, 1989; Wasser & Bresler, 1996). Each individual might at times be required to accommodate his or her perspective to the views being expressed by others, but can also make unique contributions that spur group thinking. Thus, learning occurs not only despite but also because of the existence of differing perspectives and objectives within the group. Just as failure in applying existing knowledge is seen in a constructivist view as driving individual learning, lack of consensus among individuals (i.e., *social disequilibration*) is seen as driving its development in a sociocultural perspective.

The dialogue that occurs in Minstrell's classroom—and in all mentored reflective discourses—is actively shaped by the teacher.

Furthermore, it is not typical of the discussions that usually occur in classrooms or in ordinary social interactions. As Stubbes (1983) observed,

> [T]here is a general rule in our society that demands that interaction proceed at a smooth flow: silences are often considered embarrassing and disagreements must normally be mitigated. So speakers immediately counteract departures from the smooth ongoing of normal face-to-face interactions by making (if necessary, violent) attempts to restore the ritual equilibrium. (p. 241)

In fact, learning is enhanced not by *smoothing the flow*, but by allowing long silences and working to create an atmosphere in which disagreements and differing points of view can emerge.[15] Equilibrium is not the immediate goal of the classroom conversation. The teacher, aiming to set the stage for reflective discourse, probes in ways that produce some disequilibrium for students. Given that such dialogue is at odds with what students are accustomed to, the teacher must spend considerable time establishing classroom norms. In this effort, the teacher is doing more than establishing rules unique to that classroom. Rather, in taking responsibility to lead the class in the negotiation of norms that enable reflective discourse, the teacher is acting as the students' guide into the community of science. These norms are more than a means for facilitating discussions that promote understanding; they are part and parcel of scientific thinking.

### Classroom Norms

Cobb and his associates (e.g., Cobb, Wood, & Yackel, 1989) have written extensively about the importance of establishing classroom norms to support students' mathematical thinking, and they have offered evidence of the kind of learning that can take place in such classrooms. They make the distinction between general classroom norms that might be seen in any classroom trying to encourage reflective discussion and those norms that are particular to the discipline. We provide examples of both types of norms in Table 4.3.

General norms include listening carefully to one's peers, striving to understand them, and being open to new ideas. Norms that are more specific to scientific discourse include maintaining a skeptical attitude about claims and insisting on evidence. Note

TABLE 4.3

CLASSROOM NORMS FOR SUPPORTING DISCOURSE

General Classroom Norms

- Carefully listening to one's peers
- Responsibility for understanding others' arguments, including asking for clarification from peers and the teacher
- Curiosity and openness to new ideas

Science-Specific Norms

- Skepticism and insistence on evidence
- Standards for evidence and for scientific explanations
- Valuing hypothetical reasoning ("what if?")

that there is a tension between the general norm of curiosity and openness and the scientific norm of skepticism:

> Science is characterized as much by skepticism as by openness. Although a new theory may receive serious attention, it rarely gains widespread acceptance in science until its advocates can show it is borne out by the evidence [and] explains more than rival theories. ... (American Association for the Advancement of Science, 1989, pp. 134–135)

These norms suggest that learning to engage in scientific inquiry is not simply a matter of acquiring various cognitive skills. To a large extent, these norms—values, agreements, and conventions—are at the heart of scientific inquiry and are learned within a group as members negotiate ways of communicating and working with one another in the pursuit of common objectives. Indeed, what we have called reflective discourse should not be thought of simply as a pedagogical device. Rather, science *is* a discourse, and learning to talk like a scientist *is* learning science (Rosebery & Warren, 1998).

## SUPPORTING DISCOURSE IN A NETWORKED ENVIRONMENT

We have argued that students need mentoring in how to carry on reflective discussions, and that because of the nuances of the norms that underlay these discussions this mentoring is best done by a teacher in the classroom. We acknowledge that student and teacher use of the network for substantive discussions is still relatively new and that the research is still in its infancy. There is some research that is more optimistic about the potential of online discussions to foster learning. This includes research in university courses making use of the network to promote learning through discussion (e.g., Smith & Taylor, 1995; Harasim, Hiltz, Teles, & Turoff, 1995) as well as research on efforts to establish online high school courses (Virtual High School, vhs.concord.org/). Computer Supported Intentional Learning Environments (CSILE) is a technology that supports knowledge-building discourse and communities, and it has been the subject of active research in classrooms. A key objective of the CSILE project is that of building new knowledge within educational communities. In CSILE classrooms, students' notes (written, graphical, or other) are stored in a searchable database that provides the knowledge base for the community.

Scardamalia and Bereiter (1996) saw complementarity between the written discourse fostered by the CSILE project and the oral discourse of the classroom:

> CSILE-supported classrooms have as much opportunity for oral interchange as students in other classrooms. Accordingly, CSILE-supported classrooms allow for the immediacy, spontaneity, and ease of [oral] conversation, as well as the more reflective and long-term benefits of written discourse. (p. 263)

The authors pointed to the online discourse as more conducive to reflection than oral discourse, and they supported this conclusion by noting that students using CSILE frequently comment on "the blessing of having time to think rather than needing to respond under the pressures of oral discourse" (p. 263). It is worth contrasting the in-class and online situations. In a classroom-based mentored reflective discussion, a teacher's silent pause is intentional and intended as a clear message encouraging reflection on the issue at hand. In an online discussion, the inevitable delays incurred when using online correspondence allow a student time for reflection; however, the student may or may not make use of the opportunity. Although we acknowledge that time for reflection is a potentially important affordance of online discussion, we continue to question whether the advantages of online communication can outweigh all of the disadvantages.

This section briefly outlines characteristics of curricula and staff development that we believe are necessary if this type of discourse is to become more commonplace. First, however, we want to emphasize that, in adopting a skeptical view of the role of the network in supporting reflective discourse, we are not questioning its value in realizing other objectives of network science. We have documented many examples (some of which are included in chap. 2) of teachers using the network to support and deepen their students' scientific explorations. It is helpful to look at yet another example—one that underlines the value of carefully constructed classroom collaborations to foster classroom-based discourse.

A productive relationship developed in the fall of 1996 between two elementary classrooms participating in Classroom BirdWatch. On learning that the feeder put up by Cathy Burge's class in Racine, Wisconsin, was attracting no birds, Pat Hughes' class in Harleysville, Pennsylvania, arranged to share observations and bird counts from its feeder. The Wisconsin students, in turn, read about and discussed characteristics and behaviors of birds sighted by their partner class in Pennsylvania. They wrote reports of what they had learned and sent copies of these to their partner school. Because the reports were handwritten and included student drawings, Burge sent them via regular mail. From one of these reports, the students in Pennsylvania learned that mourning doves coo. This prompted a lively discussion, and some doubt, because they had never heard any such sound; they had been watching the birds through their large classroom window. After observing outside, they e-mailed confirmation to Wisconsin that, indeed, mourning doves make cooing sounds (Burge, 1997; Hughes, 1997).

This collaboration was beneficial to both classes. Shared data and information prompted questions and further observations in one class, and in both classes, deeper discussions about bird behavior. Burge credited the collaboration for keeping her and her students involved in the bird study until birds eventually appeared at their feeder. Another teacher in her school abandoned the curriculum after a couple of birdless weeks. Although the network connection served to keep interest alive and even prompted substantive conversations, we think it significant that, according to both teachers' accounts, the in-depth discussions occurred within each of the classes, not between them.

Our reservations about using the network to engage students in reflective discussions is based not only on our observation that these discussions seldom occur over the network, but also on our assessment of the complex nature of the mentoring that we have observed in classrooms like Minstrell's. We expect that efforts directed toward enhancing the network connections between schools (e.g., by making use of synchronous communications) will do little to remedy the problem.

As mentioned in chapter 1, network science curricula, in focusing on the affordances of emerging technologies, have tended to ignore the roles of the classroom teacher and of curriculum materials in supporting teachers. Goodman Research Group (1998) reported that, although most of the network science projects evaluated view staff development as vital to their success, they lack the resources needed to provide it. Many network science curricula offer considerable background information about the science as well as suggestions about how to organize student activities, but we consistently find little pedagogic advice on how to lead the class discussion. Fruitful class discussions can be difficult to initiate and maintain because, among other reasons, they require that the teacher has established a classroom environment that allows for a style of dialogue that is atypical of classroom interactions. To guide the discussion productively, the teacher must have sufficient knowledge of the discipline, knowledge of students' intuitive reasoning, and ideas about how to bridge the two. The curricula materials often encourage teachers to lead classroom discussions but contain few if any suggestions about how to structure or moderate them. Nor do they include examples of the beliefs students are likely to hold and how teachers might respond to them. Furthermore, the learning objectives of many activities are sufficiently ambiguous that it is unclear where the discussions should go. An inexperienced teacher looking at these materials might reasonably conclude that students will spontaneously bring to classroom and online discussions a stream of useful hypotheses and explanations and that it will be obvious how to build on these ideas. Such a teacher will be disappointed and perhaps disillusioned.

In the absence of quality staff development and more supportive curricula materials, substantive classroom discussions will probably be as rare in network science classrooms as they are in traditional ones. It is to these issues—staff development and curriculum development—that we believe network science programs should turn their attention and resources. In considering the general characteristics of these materials and programs, we believe they should accommodate four general domains that classroom teachers of network science will need:

- A sound understanding of the science concepts being investigated
- Knowledge of the informal ways students currently think about the concepts being investigated
- A model for how students might build on their current understandings to develop an understanding more compatible with accepted scientific theory
- Knowledge of classroom norms that are conducive to reflective discussions and of how to establish them

Coming to see these skills and knowledge as essential requires radically transforming our view of teaching to replace our image of "teacher as technician" with "teacher as intellectual" (Little, 1993). A number of staff development efforts in both science and mathematics can serve as models of aspects of this approach. Teachers participating in Cognitively Guided Instruction (CGI), for example, spend considerable time developing models for how their students currently understand various mathematical and scientific ideas. By having teachers focus on student thinking, CGI staff developers believe they are providing more than specific information that teachers can apply in the classroom. Rather, they are using this focus as a way to shift the orientation from skill and knowledge acquisition to that of teachers as reflective practitioners (Carpenter & Franke, 1998).

One good model of how curricular materials can support teachers in leading reflective discussions is found in the elementary mathematics curriculum, *Investigations in Number, Data, and Space* (TERC, 1996). The teacher materials constitute a framework for engaging students in a discussion, including suggestions about how teachers might phrase a question, the kind of student responses they might expect, how to follow up, and, most important, the educational objectives of the discussion. The materials also include extended samples of actual class discussions along with short analyses of the decisions a teacher makes along the way. The units frequently have students working in small groups to solve a problem, often with the use of manipulatives. Collectively, the work of individual students and small groups plays a subsidiary role to the class discussions that follow.

Another curriculum that provides a helpful model is *Global Systems Science* developed by Sneider and Golden (1999) at Lawrence Hall of Science and distributed by NASA Teacher Resource Centers. These materials, aimed at high school students, provide explicit guidance for students and teachers about the norms of class discussions.

In contrast to these examples, in many network science curricula we have reviewed, the activities generally constitute the central focus, and the class discussion functions as either a supportive activity or an extension. As a result, class discussions are typically not given the time or emphasis that is required to support student learning effectively.

## SUMMARY

We offer evidence that, counter to the original vision of network science, classrooms are not using their electronic connections to carry on science-like discussions. In exploring what these discussions might ideally look like and the theoretical reasons for expecting them to play a critical role in learning science, we suggest that students require considerable support in learning how to *talk science*—more support than they are likely to find online.

The experience of the network science curricula to date has led us to doubt that virtual communities for K to 12 students can replace classroom-based communities. Our reservations are based on how difficult it has proved to get substantive discussions going among participating classrooms. These reservations have been reinforced by our analysis of class discussions, such as those in Minstrell's class. Given the timing, monitoring, nuanced voice, eye contact, and on-the-spot decision making required to engage students in reflective discussions, online discussions are a poor substitute by comparison.[16] Most simply, the necessary subtleties of face-to-face interaction have no sufficient analogue online. It would be especially unfortunate if, in our ardent attempts to help classrooms get online discussions going, we inadvertently undermined efforts to improve the quality of class discussions.

The complexity and sophistication of these various components pose a problem no less difficult than that of how to support students in the classroom: How do we support teachers who are trying to engage students in reflective classroom discussions? When faced with the costs associated with inservice teacher development, the possibility of using the Internet becomes an attractive alternative. However, the same critique offered earlier for why the Internet is ill suited for students learning the subtleties of substantive discourse applies as well to the challenge of teachers learning new pedagogies. The Internet may come to play an important role in sustaining contacts and building on experiences that take place in summer institutes, but it is a poor substitute for such experiences.[17]

We all have much to learn about online discussions. With more experience, will students and teachers develop significantly better skills for participating in and leading online discussions than they have now? Will faster connections, multimedia communication channels, and design innovations improve the results?

We acknowledge that student and teacher use of the network for substantive discussions is still relatively new and that the research is still in its infancy. However, we doubt that faster or more interactive forms of electronic communications will make a noticeable difference in the frequency and quality of networked classroom communications. Nor do we believe that online moderators will be able to play a role comparable to that of a skillful teacher in the classroom.

Furthermore, it is not that we necessarily want such discussions to occur online; rather, we want them to take place somewhere. Our contention is that the classroom is the best place for discussions to occur and the place where they are the easiest to initiate and sustain. It is within a classroom that the norms of reflective discourse can be consistently shaped by the teacher and learned by the students over the extended periods of time that are required. This being the case, the network is not the place to escape the superficiality of classroom talk, but rather the place to put critical communication skills, learned in the classroom, to work.

# 5

# Bringing Students to the Data

Imagine this: Students in Riverside, California, are analyzing data they downloaded—data that include measurements of air quality collected locally by classrooms all over the world. Looking at a scatterplot of . . . they notice. . . . Wondering whether. . . , they generate a time-series plot that shows. . . . Excited by their discovery, they e-mail a draft of their findings to collaborating students in Hobart, Australia. They, in turn. . . .

Imagine you must. Although we have read others' accounts of such happenings, in our visits to numerous network science classrooms and our searches through logs of Internet communications, we have found little that captures this level of student engagement and learning with shared data.

One of the reasons students of network science seldom analyze data is that they do not quite know where to start; they have had little experience analyzing data. This is true of their teachers as well (Russell, 1990). Eighty-four percent of the teachers surveyed by Goodman Research Group (1998) said they needed more help with teaching data analysis, and they were quick to point out their own limitations: "Interpreting data is a problem area for me" (p. 31).

Unfortunately, it will take more to solve this problem than short graphing tutorials for students and 1-week data analysis workshops for their teachers. Data analysis involves considerably more than knowing how to make and read a few graphs. There is a large body of research literature showing how difficult it is even for college students to reason statistically (see Shaughnessy, 1992, for a review). Recent research in classrooms indicates that students have trouble with fairly rudimentary ideas. Younger students do not regard data as a valid basis for beliefs (Hancock, Kaput, & Goldsmith, 1992), nor do they think of data as something they can probe for answers as they can people (Lehrer & Romberg, 1996). Mokros and Russell (1995) described conceptual difficulties that middle school students face in using means and medians to summarize data. More recent studies (e.g., Bright & Friel, 1998; Gal, Rothschild, & Wagner, 1989; Roth & Bowen, 1994; Watson & Moritz, 1998) have found that most students will not freely use means or medians to compare two groups. This is true even for high schoolers who have completed a yearlong course in probability and statistics (Konold, Pollatsek, Well, & Gagnon, 1997).

However, we are optimistic that the situation is improving—that in 10 years, students and teachers will be considerably more facile with data than they are now. One reason is that nearly every K to 12 mathematics curricula now devotes prime space to probability and statistics. This achievement can be credited in large part to the effect of NCTM's (1989) *Standards*, which granted probability and statistics a status equal to that of geometry and algebra. As a result, the mathematics education community is beefing up its efforts to improve instruction in data analysis, designing better tools, materials, and staff development. The previously mentioned problems identified in earlier research should not be taken as evidence of immutable cognitive limitations. Rather, they indicate in what ways students have difficulty given the little instruction they typically have received. An increasing number of researchers are documenting what students at various ages are able to learn with appropriate instruction. Lajoie (1998) provided an overview of how these research and development efforts are proceeding and informing one another.

Of course, network science cannot put student data analysis on hold, waiting for the situation in mathematics education to improve. First, the teaching of data analysis is not the sole domain of mathematics education. Not only is data analysis a fundamental tool of science, but the underlying processes are in many respects similar to what is characterized as the *scientific method.* Another reason to press on is that we can make some progress based on what we already know. By attending to a few simple principles in designing curriculum and selecting appropriate data and tools, we can improve students' involvement with data.

This chapter begins with an examination of the role that questions play in initiating and then guiding data analysis. As part of this discussion, we present two case studies: one of an expert analyst and the other of fourth-grade students being assisted by their teacher. We use these case studies to illustrate recommendations about how to improve the design of network science curricula. These recommendations focus on the importance of helping students frame empirical questions they care about, locate data relevant to those questions, and explore the data without losing sight of their questions.

## AN APPETITE FOR DATA

In the fall of 1997, we hiked with a class of 10th graders out to the fringe of an estuary in South Boston, Massachusetts. This was their teacher's first year using a network science curriculum. She was thrilled with the idea of students collecting real data and sharing these data with distant classrooms. The students were equipped with light meter, jerry-rigged sextant, thermometer, and blank data forms—items they needed to collect information they would send to participating classrooms. In the days prior to this, teams of three or four students had practiced using a particular apparatus, learning the protocol that would result in good measurements. Arriving on the site, the teacher gathered her students around a ledge to remind them of the obligations inherent in being part of a global, network science community.

> These measurements are going into the project data bank. Do you understand the importance of this? Students all over the world are doing the same thing as you are today. They will get different measurements than you, but the process will be the same. It's critical that you do it correctly.

However, this class, like most that uploaded their data that day, would never log back into the data bank to download. Why is this? Consider this analogous situation.

> It's potluck, and all the guests have come. It was "Hi" at the front door and "Where do you want me to put this?" as they moved through the

kitchen out the back to the pool and volleyball. Now it's time for lunch, but there's no line forming at the plate pile. You go to the back door and discover the problem: It's locked. You easily solve that problem, then announce loudly that lunch is served. After 20 minutes you're still alone in the kitchen. What's the problem now? No need to conduct a survey to figure this one out. Your guests aren't hungry enough yet.

A few years ago, we assumed that classrooms seldom downloaded data because most teachers did not have the means or know-how to access the data electronically, and we attributed the situation to the "locked door." The access problem has been largely solved. All 58 of the teachers surveyed as part of the evaluation by Goodman Research Group (1998) had access to computers—over half of them both at school and home. Seventy percent of them had access in their classroom, and the majority of these described their access as reliable. Over 80% reported using e-mail and the Web to correspond with other teachers and project staff. Most of them are a button click away from retrieving data. Again, why aren't they clicking that button?

Teachers we have asked have reported (after apologizing) that they are short on time and are not sure what to do with the data. As one of the teachers quoted in Goodman Research Group (1998) expressed it:

> I find it difficult to keep up with all of the data coming in. Time is difficult to find to properly analyze it. (p. 31)

Lack of time and skills are certainly understandable reasons for not downloading and analyzing data. We see these explanations, however, as indicators of an even deeper problem—lack of appetite. Teachers and their students have no compelling reason to look at the data.

For most people, collecting data, culling through them, and producing statistical summaries are not rewarding activities. Motivated to do so in a required course, college students often refer to their course in *Sadistics*. Listen to the explanations for their involvement in network science given by two teachers in the report by Goodman Research Group (1998):

> To have our students do exactly what real life scientists do: observe, distribute data and data analysis. (p. 25)

To teach students how to research accurately and to relay information in a scientific manner. (p. 25)

No turning up of noses at data here, but neither is there a register of excitement or a hint that data analysis is more than an operational appendage of science. What would compel one to analyze data? A person is driven to data when he or she has a problem to solve or a question that begs to be answered. Absent such motivation, analyzing data is simply a chore.

Later in the chapter, we offer several suggestions about how to draw students into data analysis and keep them engaged. First, however, we describe the nature of data analysis and examine how questions not only motivate our search of data but also direct us where and how to look.

## The Iterative Nature of Data Analysis

Statistical practice has recently undergone some dramatic changes. Twenty years ago, it was standard to design a study with a specific hypothesis in mind, collect the data, run statistical tests hoping to find results significant at the $p < .05$ level, publish the results, and never look any closer than that at the data. In fact, statisticians discourage *snooping* in the data for other than predicted results—although such fishing expeditions turn up interesting findings, many of them are only due to chance variation.

Beginning in the late 1960s, the statistician John Tukey was among those who began arguing that it was silly to use data only to test theories. Why not also use data to help generate new ideas, to search for the unexpected? Certainly scientists could be trusted to remember that findings culled from these explorations require further questioning and testing. To assist in this process, Tukey articulated principles for flexibly exploring data and developed plotting techniques for visually detecting patterns and trends in raw data. However, plotting large amounts of data by hand in the ways he recommended was so time-consuming that few followed his admonitions. Computers have changed that. We now have the means not only to access volumes of data but also to analyze them visually and flexibly in truly exploratory ways.

Tukey's (1977) view of Exploratory Data Analysis contrasts with an often propagated and misleading idealization of science: generate a research hypothesis, collect some data, analyze the data to either confirm or disconfirm the hypothesis, and form appropriate conclusions. This idealization reinforces various misconceptions about science, among them that all hypotheses are well formed before scientists collect data and that they do not explore data after the fact by searching for unexpected results. The misleading idealization also encourages the view of data analysis as a recipe that experts use to extract *right* answers from a set of data.

As Tukey's work has made clear, data analysis (and the scientific process more generally) is in reality a complex collection of judgments, perceptions, abstractions, hypothetical reasoning, and critical thinking. Experts draw on their vast experience, knowledge, and honed skills to guide their initial choice of questions and, once analysis has begun, to change course when needed. On the one hand, their initial questions, including which data to collect and how to code them, are shaped partly by their knowledge of their statistical tool kit. On the other hand, they know that much research is exploratory and that vague hypotheses become clarified only in the course of examining the data. Investigators' initial hypotheses guide the early stages of the investigation. However, as soon as they begin looking at data, they often modify these questions or abandon them for better ones.

Thus, neither scientific investigation nor data analysis is a linear process where the investigator fixes on a question and then searches for its answer. Rather, they are iterative processes—back and forth dialogues between hunches and what the data reveal. Current hunches (guesses, ideas, hypotheses) guide the exploration of the data—what data values investigators inspect, how they display those values, and what they look for in those displays. What they find in the data, in turn, often prompts them to revise their thinking and ask different questions. With these new hunches, they return to look at the same data in new ways or perhaps search for additional, more relevant data.

### Case Study: Analysis of Atmospheric $CO_2$

To show how questions guide the exploration of data and how, in turn, they are modified as a result of those explorations, we examine an account we recently received from a colleague, Bill Finzer (1997). Finzer was working with a partner analyzing data as part of an activity that a curriculum designer had developed and was now piloting for classroom use. They were using the analysis tool *Fathom.*

Finzer is an experienced data analyst.[18] Thus, in many ways, this episode is uncharacteristic of what we would expect of students in the classroom. Our purposes for the moment, however, are to exemplify the iterative nature of data analysis and to show how guided explorations can turn into more open-ended ones. This example is revealing because in it Finzer describes not only what he and his partner found while analyzing data on $CO_2$ emissions, but also thoughts and questions that arose during analysis.

The topic for the evening was $CO_2$ emissions and exploring time series data. In the first part of the meeting, we looked at $CO_2$ in the atmosphere as measured at the Mauna Keo volcano in Hawaii. We could see the $CO_2$ really [was] increasing. And, even scarier, increasing at an increasing rate!

We began by trying to describe the data and then to estimate rate of increase. The questions we were asked [in the pilot curriculum unit] were open-ended enough that we found ourselves asking lots of our own questions and coming up with our own methods. Time flew by! ... The data show[ed] a strong seasonal variation on top of a general increase.

We wanted to see just the seasonal variation, which we did by plotting $CO_2$ versus month, and then just the general increase, which we did by plotting $CO_2$ versus year and filtering out all but January.

Once we got an estimate of rate of increase, we tried to use it to interpolate and then extrapolate. It really hit home that extrapolation [was] dangerous! It assume[d] the inevitable, but we knew that the folks at the Kyoto conference had just come up with an agreement for reducing greenhouse gas emissions.

At the end of the session, we had 5 or 10 minutes to look at another collection—carbon production by region and year. We plotted total carbon versus year [Fig. 5.1].[19]

This was really amazing. Because data for 10 regions are there for each year, the plot separated itself into one line of points for each region. ... Expected, but still striking was seeing our [North America]

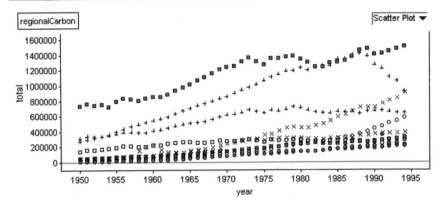

**FIG. 5.1. Annual carbon emissions (in metric tons) by region.**

carbon production way at the top. But then there was this line of dots coming up to and reaching ours in the mid-1980s, and then falling way off starting in 1989. What could this be? Centrally planned Europe! The dissolution of the Soviet Union and subsequent economic collapse led to a huge falloff in carbon production!

This was fascinating, but the most surprising discovery [my partner] and I made had to do with "flaring." You may ask, "What is flaring?" Well, it's carbon production that occurs when oil wells burn the gases that vent off from the well rather than attempt to store them up. It's a small part of total carbon production. Looking at the Middle East total carbon production, we found this strong blip in 1991 [Fig. 5.2].

"What's going on?" we asked. Wasn't that the year of the Gulf War? If this blip is because of the war, shouldn't we see a lot of flaring from the Middle East in that year? Sure enough, the flaring graph, made by plotting flaring versus year and selecting Middle East in the bar chart, showed the blip even stronger!

We were excited and had to share our discoveries with the rest of the group. The time was up, but we could see that there were many other interesting features to explore in this flaring graph.

Finzer's account illustrates how the data analysis engine is fueled by questions. A back and forth exchange ensued between his hunches and what he learned from the data. At times, hunches led the way, directing him and his partner to look for specific patterns. At other times, surprises in the data led to new

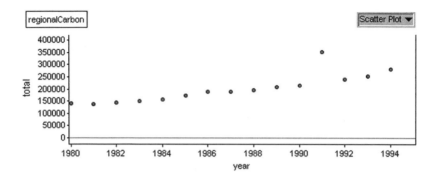

**FIG. 5.2. Annual total carbon emissions (metric tons) in the Middle East.**

questions and hunches. This interplay is most evident when Finzer surmised that the surprising blip in the 1991 data for the Middle East resulted from the Gulf War, which led them to locate and analyze data on flaring. This is data analysis at its best—a perpetual motion machine driven in turn by hunches and unexpected patterns found in the data.

## GETTING DATA ANALYSIS GOING

Without assistance, few high school students working with these data would be able to proceed at Finzer's level of sophistication. Finzer knew the analysis software he was working with and could draw on his knowledge of recent world events to generate plausible explanations for the trends they found. We suggest, however, that given the right data, tools, and teacher support, even young students can reason about data in an iterative style. Before offering several suggestions about how to get students started on data analysis, we look at another case study in which a teacher helped his students formulate suitable questions and analyze relevant data.

### Case Study: Tracking Bald Eagles

This account comes from Bob Coulter, who at the time was a fourth-grade teacher in St. Louis, Missouri.[20] Students in his class paired up to conduct a research project in which they selected a researchable question, analyzed available data, and drew conclusions. Previous to this, they had worked as a whole class tracking the migrations of monarch butterflies via the Journey North web site. The previous year, the same students had also participated in Journey North's study of the blooming of tulips.

This retrospective report gives us some insights into the kind of assistance needed by students new to data analysis. Coulter provided a structure that allowed the students to take on a complex task that was technically beyond their ability. He did this by assisting them where they needed help but otherwise allowing them to do what they were capable of doing. We see Coulter helping his students select and refine appropriate questions, but not giving them the questions; prompting them to generate explanations for what they observe, but not explaining the data for them; and pointing them to other data sources to test their explanations, but letting them analyze those data and draw their own conclusions. From the perspective of Lave and Wenger (1991), Coulter's mentoring allowed these novices to apply and generalize what they knew while learning additional aspects of data analysis as they engaged, with his assistance, in a legitimate scientific investigation.

> The students' first task was to generate a question they could pursue. After exploring a number of possibilities I had listed on the board, Zach and Paul chose to investigate the migration of bald eagles. They had seen other types of eagles locally, as the raptors' Midwest wintering ground was only 20 miles north of St. Louis. The opportunity to track eagles online through Journey North was one of the aspects of this question that attracted them.
>
> In the spring of 1998, Journey North tracked three eastern and four western bald eagles. By accessing weekly updates of their positions online and downloading this information into NGS Works, Zach and Paul were able to study the movement of individual eagles from late March through mid-May as the birds moved north from wintering grounds to their spring nesting sites [www.learner.org/jnorth/spring1998/critters/]. Because of time limitations, I encouraged the student to focus their attention on only two of the eagles. They selected eagle #5 on the West coast and #F42 on the East. With my assistance, they narrowed their question to seeing if there were any differences in the migration behavior of the eastern and western eagles.

Early in the project, Zach and Paul made weekly maps in NGS Works showing the location of each eagle. These locations shifted a bit from week to week, but basically showed each eagle nesting in one general location. The students noticed a significant difference, however, by visually comparing latitudes on the map they had made—the western eagle seemed to be nesting farther north than the eastern eagle. To see whether this observation held for the other five eagles tracked by Journey North, I suggested they consult the data tables on the Journey North site, which listed the weekly latitude and longitude coordinates of each eagle. By comparing the latitudes, they confirmed that all of the western eagles were wintering farther north than the eastern eagles.

I challenged the students to explain this observation. After some consideration, they mentioned possible differences in habitat and weather. Because information on habitat was not readily available, I encouraged them to explore possible differences in weather between the eastern and western coastlines. They quickly asserted that the west coast was warmer than the east coast. In making this argument they referred to maps from Journey North the past two years, tracking the blooming of red emperor tulip bulbs. Zach and Paul participated in this project last year, and students in other classes were continuing this study by comparing last year's results with this year's data. The maps showed the dates on which tulips bloomed in the spring for 1997 and 1998 for participating classrooms all over the United States. They chose a few sites on each coast and verified that tulips on the west coast tended to bloom earlier than those at the same latitude on the east coast. This was not a new observation for them, as we had had similar discussions the previous year.

I challenged them to go even further. Could they verify that the temperatures differed along the two coasts? To pursue this question, I helped them locate climatological data in almanacs and online (through Accu-Weather). By comparing data for New York City and Seattle, which were the two major cities closest to the eagles' locations, they were able to verify that, at least in this case, the west coast city was warmer during some winter months even though it was at a higher latitude than its east coast counterpart. This was counterintuitive, but a great expansion of the students' thinking about latitude and temperature. The weather data also proved to be quite helpful in supporting Zach and Paul's explanation of the eagle's migration patterns. (see Table 5.1).

Feeling content with their justification, Zach and Paul continued tracking their two eagles. As the spring progressed, the western eagle left its wintering grounds earlier and traveled farther north than did the eastern eagle. This time without assistance, the students checked to see if this same pattern was true for the other eagles tracked by Journey North, and in general, it was.

Seeing from their data that these were general behavior trends and not just an aberration, Zach and Paul concluded that western eagles wintered farther north, left their wintering grounds a few weeks earlier than eastern eagles, and headed farther north in the spring. Based on their background reading about eagles, they speculated that this pattern was largely due to differences in weather, which they thought might affect food availability, especially if northern lakes were frozen.

TABLE 5.1

AVERAGE HIGH AND LOW TEMPERATURES FOR SEATTLE
AND NEW YORK CITY, JANUARY–APRIL 1998

| Month | Seattle Hi/Low | New York City Hi/Low |
| --- | --- | --- |
| January | 45/36 | 37/24 |
| February | 48/37 | 38/24 |
| March | 52/39 | 45/30 |
| April | 58/43 | 57/42 |

In this example, we see again how data analysis was preceded by a question the students cared about and how that question changed as a result of what they observed. New questions prompted them to look at the same data differently and to search for additional data.

In this case, a teacher played a critical role and, in so doing, drew on a rich background of knowledge.[21] Coulter would have had little idea about when and how to assist the students had he no experience with fourth graders or with the use of student projects (see Polman, in press),[22] scant knowledge of data analysis, or a weak understanding of the science content. Specifically, had Coulter not helped focus the students' initial research project into one that compared eastern and western eagles, the students may never have noticed the difference in latitude of the birds' wintering sites. This simple observation prompted a series of additional questions. We suggest herein a number of principles, several of which are evident in both the Coulter and Finzer case studies, that educators can use to help students begin analyzing data.

## Asking Questions That Data Can Answer

Questions that can be answered with data are often referred to as *empirical questions*. This is a novel idea for many students. Ask young students to pose a research question and they will typically generate a question whose answer they could find in a book— What is acid rain? How do volcanoes make lava? Where do monarchs go in the winter? Similarly, if students are asked questions that could be answered by analyzing data—How much rain do we get in Seattle? How acidic is our rain?—they are likely to interpret them as questions that have already been answered. To them, research is locating answers in books or asking experts. Indeed, most of the research even college students are asked to do is typically of this sort. Given this set of expectations, students need guidance in coming to understand that they can answer many questions not by asking experts but by collecting and analyzing relevant data.

*Querying Data.* In their classroom study of fifth graders, Lehrer and Romberg (1996) worked with students to design a survey of student interests. Among other things, the survey asked students to list their favorite school subject, favorite winter sport, and how many hours they spent watching TV. After they had administered the survey, Lehrer and Romberg asked the students to come up with questions that they could ask about the data. To these fifth graders, this request was ridiculous. Questions, they countered, could be posed to people, but certainly not to data. Lehrer and Romberg prompted the students with various examples, such as, "Which is the least favorite school subject?" The students successfully used these examples to generate a list of similar questions. However, they needed further assistance to see that they could answer some of these by analyzing the data they had just obtained. Their first thought was to conduct another survey using these new questions.

In analyzing data, we organize and summarize data to reveal patterns and trends that otherwise remain invisible. Students need help coming to understand that data are not just a collection of results from which they can directly read off useful information. Rather, they must learn to ask questions of the data.

*Narrowing the Inquiry.* In the Journey North case study, Coulter helped the students both limit their questions and make them more specific. With his assistance, Paul and Zach modified their original idea of "studying the movement of individual eagles" to asking, "Are there differences in the migration behavior of eastern eagles and western eagles?" and finally, "Do western eagles winter farther north than eastern eagles?" This last question was one that could be directly answered with the data they had.

Curriculum materials often suggest that students generate a list of possible research questions or hypotheses. This is a good technique for getting students to explore alternatives. It is also an opportunity for the teacher to help students formulate empirical questions. However, before students begin analyzing data, they should have in mind only one major question. Generally, the more specific the question, the better.

*Basing Questions on Data.* For students, coming to view data as a source of belief is a high hurdle. We have observed college students present various graphs and statistics on some issue and then go on to offer as a conclusion their own opinion—an opinion often contradicted by the data they presented. In their classroom studies with fifth to eighth graders, Hancock, Kaput, and Goldsmith (1992) reported that most students did not expect that "collecting and analyzing data might yield knowledge that is more reliable than their own personal judgment" (p. 356). After a year-long teaching experiment, these researchers reported some progress in helping students develop this perspective. Such a perspective could be added to the list of science-specific norms that we offered in Table 4.3. That is, we can view the development of *data as knowledge source* as a cultural practice that is formulated as students participate with the teacher in making empirical claims and supporting those claims not only with logical arguments, demonstrations, and examples but also with observations that have been coded as data—as measurements, counts, or categories.

*Predicting What the Data Will Show.* Many believe that to remain objective a scientist should not speculate on an issue until after examining the data. In fact, scientists typically have strong expectations even before they collect data. Scientists are objective not because they are free of opinions, but because they hold their opinions subject to empirical refutation. Students as well as scientists are better off if they have specific expectations about what they will observe before looking at data. Here are three reasons why:

First, predictions motivate. Just as most of us are more emotionally engaged watching a sporting event when we care who wins, we are more eager to look at data when we think we know what the data will show. Finzer's excitement came largely from confirming his speculation regarding the cause of the sudden increase in carbon production in the Middle East. As described in chapter 4, before weighing an object in a vacuum, Minstrell asked his students to predict what they would observe. After voicing their predictions, the students were personally invested in the outcome of the experiment especially because they held a variety of conflicting views. When students predict beforehand what they will find, they have a compelling reason to look at data.

Second, predictions direct our attention. An expectation or prediction lets us know what we are looking for; it primes us to detect patterns or differences that might otherwise escape our notice. Finzer's expectation about the flaring data led him to the particular data and informed him precisely what he was looking for—a spike in 1991. At one point in their investigation, Zach and Paul went to the Journey North web site to compare the latitudes of nesting sites of western and eastern eagles. These latitudes were not radically different. Had they not expected to find higher latitudes for the western eagles, they may have never noticed them. When we look at data expecting to see nothing in particular, that is usually what we see. Contrary to what we might assume, having an expectation prepares us not only to uncover supporting patterns, but also to be surprised by findings that run counter to our predictions (Konold, 1995).

Third, predictions highlight theories. By asking students to predict whether an object would weigh more or less in a vacuum than in air, Minstrell elicited his students' theories about weight. It is these theories, and not the predictions themselves, that Minstrell wanted his students to focus on. It was for this same reason that Coulter was not satisfied when Zach and Paul had concluded that western eagles wintered farther north than eastern eagles. He challenged them to explain why. At this point, the students began exploring factors such as temperature patterns that might account for their observations. Thus, predictions motivate and prime students to detect patterns. In making predictions, students must draw on their theories and beliefs. It is their theories that they ultimately put to the test when they examine data.

*Striking While the Iron Is Hot.* The best time to analyze data is immediately after students have made predictions and offered reasons for those predictions. In many network science classrooms, a week or more can pass between the time when students collect and submit data and when cross-classroom data are available for analysis. Students may have been excited about the data when they collected them. However, a week later, they may no longer remember the question, and the excitement may have long since fizzled. At that point, a teacher could try to reengage the students in the same discussion, but the issue is likely to seem old hat the second time around. In such cases, it would be better to wait until data are available for analysis to engage students in deep discussions about what they expect to observe.

## KEEPING DATA ANALYSIS ON TRACK

We have discussed ways to motivate students to download and begin analyzing data. Obviously, this is only the first step. How can teachers help students sustain these investigations?

In thinking about this question, it is instructive to look back at the two case studies we examined and think about why each worked so well. Neither investigation would have continued for long if those analyzing the data came to believe the numbers had been concocted. We emphasize this point because many early advocates of network science assumed that students would be motivated and engaged once they had real data about serious issues. If we have learned anything from our experience to date in network science, it is that authentic data are not enough. Note that in the two case studies we examined, the data were more than authentic; they were there when the investigators needed them, were comprehensible to the investigators, and contained some interesting trends. Furthermore, the investigators had relevant background knowledge to draw on in explaining the patterns they found. Either analysis would probably have ground to a halt had the investigators needed data that were hard to get, had they been using unfamiliar statistical plots, or had they not found discernible or explainable patterns.

We do not mean to suggest that data analysis should, or ever does, proceed without hitches. Investigators always encounter difficulties in the course of analyzing data, and their desire to know pushes them on. However, every desire has its limits, and each additional glitch brings them closer to throwing up their hands. In designing curricula for students, educators need to identify possible breakdown points, eliminate those they can, and provide extra support when the going gets tough.

Looking across a range of network science curricula, we see the same problems time and again. Too often students are working with contexts foreign to them, with plots they struggle to interpret, and with data short on interesting trends and so full of errors that even these trends are hopelessly masked.

The remainder of this chapter offers several recommendations about the types of data and statistical displays appropriate for students. To illustrate the types of difficulties students face, we refer to data we analyzed from EnergyNet and Global Lab.[23] EnergyNet data included information from 47 schools in Illinois submitted during the 1996–1997 school year. Students collected these data as part of an energy audit of their school building. Each classroom was asked to collect 50 data values including building occupancy; floor space; R-values of roofs, walls, windows, and doors; and energy expenditures. In the case of Global Lab, we analyzed data students collected in the fall of 1997 as part of the "Snapshot" activity, which we briefly described in chapter 4 (see TERC, 1997). The data included for each of 34 schools—latitude and longitude, air temperature, sun angle, and light intensity—all measured at each site at astronomical noon on the autumnal equinox.

## Features of Data Intended for Students

*Minimal Errors.*  Unlike the data that Finzer or the Journey North students analyzed, many network science curricula make use of data collected locally by fellow students. One advantage of using student-collected data is that, as a result of collecting them, the students know quite a bit about the data even before they begin analysis. The major drawback, according to EnergyNet staff, is that such data:

usually are not accurate enough. And because of the inaccuracies in the data, the role of analyzing data, very unfortunately, has had to be downplayed. (Goodman Research Group, 1998, p. 61)

The current practice in both EnergyNet and Global Lab is to post data they receive from participating classrooms without checking for accuracy. These data tend to be riddled with errors. Some believe that such errors should be left to the students to correct. They argue that the errors are part of what makes the data authentic and that, in any case, students need to learn how to search for and remove errant data. We have seen cases in which teachers were able to take good advantage of the errors in these data. Walters (1996) reported on two EnergyNet teachers whose students developed a sense of pride in their role as sticklers for accuracy.

Unfortunately, the number of errors in student data can be overwhelming. This interrupts the flow of the investigation and requires considerable time and skill to detect. Two trained researchers spent 2 hours grooming data from the Global Lab Equinox unit of fall 1997 before we could begin analyzing them. The 1996–1997 EnergyNet data required 8 hours of checking and editing entries. Some errors were easy to spot—according to one EnergyNet school, the nuclear plant from which they claimed to get power was built in 1910. However, many problems were uncovered through comparing values on different variables to reveal inaccuracies. Dividing floor space by number of students, for example, revealed schools with as many as 400 square feet per student and as few as 10 square feet.

Data submitted by students should be checked for accuracy before they are made available to other classes. Furthermore, we suggest that project staff post archival data sets from previous years from which blatant errors have been purged. Not only can these be used for analyses, but students can compare measurements they have obtained with entries from prior years and in this way check the reasonableness of their data before submitting them.

*Salient Trends.* Real data analysis is a bit like prospecting for gold—for every nugget found, there is a small mountain of sifted refuse. In introducing students to data analysis, we should not send them off into unknown terrain with the promise of rich returns. Data students analyze should include salient trends and differences. The $CO_2$ data that Finzer analyzed had been selected by a curriculum developer in part because these were rich in trends. Had there been little of interest in the data, we would not have gotten an excited report from Finzer. Similarly, Coulter expected different migratory patterns of western and eastern eagles when he encouraged his students to compare the two.

*Familiar Contexts.* If data analysis is a dialogue between hunches and data, then analyzing data about novel phenomena is like conversing in a foreign language. The more remote those data are from our experience, the slower the conversation. In selecting data for students, we need to take into account how much the students already know about a topic.

Finzer's excitement came from relating what he found in the data to what he already knew. It was this prior knowledge that directed his search for particular variables and set the stage for observing trends in the data. This knowledge included not only rudimentary understanding of the causes and consequences of atmospheric $CO_2$, but of world geography and recent international events. Lacking this knowledge, Finzer and his partner would likely have not found themselves "asking lots of [their] own questions."

In network science curricula, by contrast, students are too often working with data that are meaningless to them. In the Global Lab Snapshot activity, the primary data are measurements of light intensity. The concept is not unfamiliar. Students know that daylight varies in brightness, and they can name factors that affect how bright the day is. However, in this activity, they measure light intensity with a digital light probe whose units are millivolts. Using a conversion table, they then change millivolts into watts per square meter. These are meaningless units to most of us. What does 925 watts per square meter look like, and is it a believable value given that the reporting school was on the 44th parallel and it was a clear day?

Turning our attention to the EnergyNet data, we presume that students can draw on their experiences to reason about things such as energy costs and speculate about how such cost might be affected by leaving lights on or doors open. However, few high school students have intuitions about what a reasonable electric bill might be for a home, let alone a school building. Before they could intelligently analyze the data, they would need to develop these sorts of intuitions.

Several elementary school network science curricula have students measure pH levels of local streams. If the idea of acidity was not itself a reach, the logarithmic scale on which it is measured would certainly place it on a high shelf. Yet the curriculum instructs students to calculate arithmetic means of multiple water samples—an activity that takes them into yet a higher realm of abstraction. Data like these can prevent even highly motivated students from engaging in thoughtful analysis.

Data are not just numbers; they are measures or codings of some phenomena. In Moore's (1992) words, they are "numbers with a context" (p. 15). If students are to find and explain trends in the data, they must keep in mind where the numbers come from and what they express. The Journey North fourth graders easily handled the data when these were presented as locations on a map. With the data in this form, they noticed that one eagle was farther north than the other. Had they been looking only at the global coordinates posted on the Journey North web page, this difference would probably have escaped their notice. Thus, even for fairly intuitive notions such as location, brightness, or school size, the process of measuring or classifying can nonetheless make the data remote. Conventions for quantifying or coding values constitute part of the meaning that must be carried with the data. Thus, we need not only involve students in explorations of phenomena with which the students have some familiarity, but also ensure that students understand how to turn observations of events into numbers and codings.

## Plots Appropriate for Students

The previous section looked at features of data that can pose difficulties for students once they begin analysis. If data are unfamiliar, full or errors, or lack salient trends, students may quickly abandon their search. This section examines how features of the data displays and summaries that students use can also thwart meaningful analysis.[24] Ironically, the same properties of statistical plots that make them suitable for detecting statistical trends make it difficult for novices to see how the data are encoded in the plots.

Roth and Bowen (1994) adapted the idea of *cascade of inscriptions* to describe how, as we present data via maps, lists, graphs, and finally equations, we move from more concrete to more abstract statistical representations. As we move along this cascade, individual data are progressively aggregated. This aggregation allows the expert to perceive ever more general features of the data at the expense of being able to identify individual data values. It is easy to forget, however, the learning required to interpret the more abstract statistical plots. As a result, we often encourage students to use plots and summaries before they sufficiently understand them and, by doing so, effectively pull the rug from beneath them.

To illustrate this progression of ever more abstract representations, we show several alternative displays of January snowfall accumulations in 20 U.S. cities. These data (Williams, 1995), include 11 cities located near the 39th parallel and 9 cities near the 47th parallel.

Note that the data are fairly concrete. They would be suitable for quite young students, at least with respect to criteria we have specified. Students could easily visualize snow piled 6 inches high. They generally know that it is colder the farther north one goes and could use this intuition to predict differences in snowfall in the two groups. The difference in the data is not subtle: The majority of cities near the 47th parallel had more than 10 inches, whereas none of the cities near the 39th parallel had that much snow.

One way to compare the two groups is to display them as *case-value bar graphs* (see Fig. 5.3). This is perhaps the most common type of graph used by newspapers. Each bar in the graph shows the value of the variable ("inches of snowfall") for a particular case (city). Cities along the 47th parallel are grouped in the upper part of the plot and ordered by amount of snowfall.

Using this plot, we can more easily compare the values of the two groups than if the data were simply listed in a table. If we rotated the plot 90 degrees, we could imagine the bars as columns of snow that fell on each particular city.

Figure 5.4 shows the same data displayed as two *stack plots* (also referred to as *line plots*). Each case is represented in this plot with a small square located on the horizontal axis to show its value. We could make a stack plot by placing a ruler vertically at the end of each bar in the case-value bar graph and marking the length of the bar near the horizontal axis. We could also make a stack plot with sticky notes or build a graph using small blocks.

By stacking cases of the same value, the stack plot gives a slightly different perspective on the data than the case-value bar graph. The stack plot shows how the cases distribute themselves

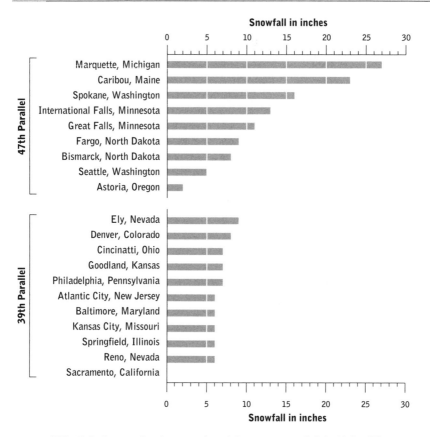

**FIG. 5.3. Case-value bar graphs of January snowfall in U.S. cities along the 39th and 47th parallels.**

over the range of possible values. We can see that for cities along the 47th parallel the snowfall accumulations are quite variable—the values are spread out fairly evenly over the range. By contrast, there is relatively little variability in accumulations for cities along the 39th parallel. With the exception of Sacramento, which had no snowfall, the values are all clustered between 6 and 9.

Figure 5.5 shows the same data displayed as two *histograms*. The histogram groups cases together into equal-sized intervals. In this histogram, the intervals are five units (inches) in width, but they can be any width we choose. As we change interval width, however, the appearance of the histogram also changes.

The height of the each bar in the histogram shows the number (frequency) of cases in that interval. Thus, histograms, like stack

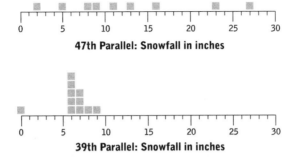

**FIG. 5.4. Stack plots of January snowfall in U.S. cities along the 39th and 47th parallels.**

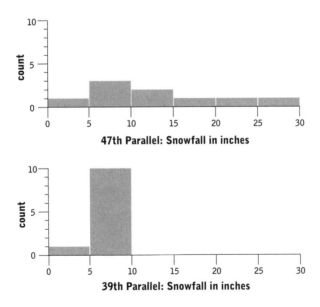

**FIG. 5.5. Histogram of January snowfall in U.S. cities along the 39th and 47th parallels.**

plots, are frequency graphs. Analogous to stepping back from a painting where we were looking at the brush stokes to now take in the whole scene, the histogram can in some instances provide a better sense than the stack plot of the overall shape of the distribution of values. This perspective is especially useful when the number of cases we are considering become numerous.

Finally, the data are displayed in Fig. 5.6 as two *box plots*.[25] This display provides summary information that is not directly available in the previous plots. The length of the rectangular box, also called the *interquartile range*, is often used to summarize the spread of the data. Its length in the upper box plot dwarfs by comparison that of the lower plot, making the differences in the variability of the two groups even more pronounced. The vertical lines within the boxes (at the left edge of the box in the lower plot) show the location of the median of each group—a measure of center not represented in any of the previous plots. For those who understand what medians and *interquartile ranges* are, and how they effectively summarize a group of values, this representation provides a quick way to compare the two sets of data.

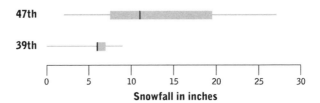

**FIG. 5.6. Box plots of January snowfall in U.S. cities along the 39th and 47th parallels.**

As we have pointed out, these various plots reveal different qualities of the data. As we move from the case-value bar graph to the stack plot and finally to the histogram and box plot, we actually lose information about individual cases. In the case-value bar graph, we see the snowfall values for each individual city. Displayed in this way, students could use their visual abilities to establish, for example, that Spokane had about twice the snowfall as Fargo. Thus, for most students, the case-value plot is an easy data representation to work with—perhaps even better than a table listing the values and cities.

In the stack plot, we still see individual cases, but we no longer know to which city they belong. Furthermore, we have to keep in mind that each plot symbol is a measurement and that its value is determined by sighting down to the scale on the x axis. For these reasons, the stack plot tends to be a little harder than the case-value graph for young students to interpret.

In the histogram and box plot, we no longer can identify individual values. Someone looking at the histogram for the cities along the 47th parallel would know that three of them had snowfalls between 5 and 9 inches. However, they would not know whether they were all 5 inches or whether the cases were distributed evenly in the interval. That information is sacrificed for a more global view of the shape of the data. In return for losing this information about individual cases, we get a better sense of group characteristics—how the data cluster and spread out. Although this is helpful information to the experienced eye, students can become disoriented as the plots they are using begin including less and less information about individual cases. This is one reason that histograms, box plots, and means are not ordinarily used in the early grades. Younger students need considerable experience before they can use such representations meaningfully (Bright & Friel, 1998; Mokros & Russell, 1995).

## A Framework for Task Selection

This section provides a framework that integrates issues discussed earlier regarding choice of data and representational tools. We hope this framework is useful to teachers and curriculum designers in choosing and creating tasks and environments for students at various levels of statistical sophistication.

Figure 5.7 lists along the horizontal axis various statistical plots, including those discussed previously. These plots are ordered from left to right according to how easy it is for students to read and identify individual case values.

Although certainly other features of plots affect their interpretability, the ease with which cases can be identified is, by itself, a powerful predictor of the abstractness of a representation. The order of plots along the horizontal axis of Figure 5.7 predicts fairly well the first appearance of these plots in the mathematics curriculum. The order also concurs with results from research by

Bright and Friel (1998), who have studied students' abilities to interpret various types of plots. The major educational implication is straightforward. Although there is power to be gained by using representations listed toward the right-hand side of Fig. 5.7, using them puts students at risk of losing their grounding. Thus, most of our introductions, even with students in the upper grades, should begin with representations on the left-hand side.

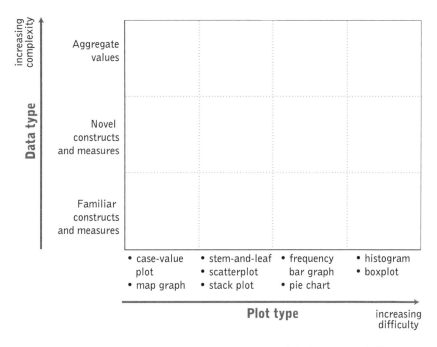

FIG. 5.7. Two dimensions of difficulty: Data and their representations.

We emphasize that this recommendation concerns where instruction should begin—not where it should end. Students have a tendency when analyzing data to attend to values of individual cases rather than to group characteristics (Hancock, Kaput, & Goldsmith, 1992; Konold et al., 1997). Students often ignore differences between group medians and instead base decisions about whether two groups differ on the location of extreme values. It could be argued that representations that highlight individual cases at the expense of group features, such as shape and dispersion, do little to develop statistical thinking. However, having students trying to reason from displays such as histograms often does little more than confuse them. We should not encourage students to use such representations until we have established the need to base decisions on group trends.

How difficult it is to reason about data represented in a statistical plot depends not only on the nature of the plot but also on the data being portrayed. Increasing levels of data complexity are depicted on the vertical axis in Fig. 5.7. Inches of snowfall is an example of a construct and measurement that would be fairly accessible to most students. Data become more difficult for students to reason about when the data involve measurements of unfamiliar constructs (e.g., insulation R value as used in EnergyNet), novel measurement units and/or scales (e.g., pH), or aggregate values (e.g., yearly electric use per student).[26]

In general, we should design introductory activities that fall in the lower left of the matrix in Fig. 5.7. This is true even for high school students with little formal exposure to statistics. Furthermore, when the science content is particularly difficult, beginning with simple statistical displays and constructs is even more important. Imagine, for example, the added difficulty Minstrell's students (see chap. 4) would have faced had he pursued the question about the effect of air pressure on weight by having students make multiple observations and average them. This would have required them to reason simultaneously about two difficult constructs—the meaning of an average and the nature of a vacuum. Similarly, when introducing students to new statistical displays and ideas, the introductory activities should involve science content and data that are relatively well understood.

Journey North is one of the more successful projects at involving students in data analysis. Note that most of the activities they support fall in the lower left of the matrix in Fig. 5.7. As with the eagle data we referred to earlier, most of the investigations they sponsor involve data that can be represented as locations on a map of North America. Given the concrete nature of the data and students' familiarity with the map of North America, students can draw on what they already know to predict or explain what might cause a bird to change direction during a migratory flight, for example. Furthermore, students are not suddenly overwhelmed with a mass of data. Each week, a few new values are added to the data set. This gives students the chance to build gradually on their understandings and interpretations. To help students raise questions, Journey North also poses questions to students on its web site and later posts a sample of student answers. Thus, not all of the responsibility of raising or answering questions is left to students or their teacher, and a model is provided for the kinds of questions that can engage students' reasoning.

Roth and Bowen's (1994) idea of *cascade of inscriptions* points to how successive representations become more complex but also suggests how we might introduce students to a new plot by helping them see how they could create it from a plot they already understand. This technique was used earlier in the chapter when we suggested that a stack plot could be made by projecting the ends of the bars of a case-magnitude plot down onto the x axis. Cobb (1998) reported recent success in teaching data analysis to middle school students: Students, supported by data analysis software, were asked to spend time using case-value plots to explore data that are naturally displayed as the length of bars (length of lizards, braking distance, hours of service from a battery). After a couple of weeks working only with this plot, students were introduced to the stack plot by first relating it to the case-magnitude plot. During 8 weeks of instruction, these were the only representations that students used.[27] Because they were not spending considerable time learning newer and more abstract representations and could keep in mind the meaning of the data, the students could focus their class discussions on more substantive issues.

## SUMMARY

The fundamental premise of network science is that students can undertake science-like investigations by sharing locally collected data with student collaborators at different geographical locations. Data collected at any site may be of limited value, but by pooling observations collected over a wide variety of sites, students can work with data that are not only real but also potentially relevant to an important question. Those of us who believed that task authenticity and student ownership of data would motivate students to analyze data they collected were quickly disabused of these notions. Helping students and teachers analyze data is now widely viewed as one of the difficult issues with which network science must struggle.

The difficulties—lack of classroom time, lack of access to appropriate tools, error-full data, complexity of data analysis, lack of support in the curriculum, and teachers with little prior data analysis experience—can seem overwhelming. All of these problems can be better understood and systematically approached by envisioning data analysis as a process that is guided at every turn by a real-world question and that requires that we remain grounded in our understanding of the data.

The primary reason network science classrooms do not download data is that students do not have relevant questions they want answered. Thus, helping students raise such questions should be our first priority. However, students will not persist if they have difficulty locating appropriate data, if the data they do locate is meaningless to them, if they do not understand the plots and statistics they use in analysis, or if they can find little of interest in the data. Nearly every problem associated with getting students to download data and keeping them engaged in analysis ultimately stems from students not making or losing the connection between the data they have and a real-world question. This being the case, the solution to most of the problems can be found in focusing on how to make and maintain these connections.

Part III

# Looking Forward

# The Internet and Classroom Learning

**I** n Part I, we examined the state of the art of network science. We began with a history of the ideas that initially motivated the development of NGS Kids Network, the first network science curriculum, and assessed these ideas based on the last decade of implementation. We then presented case studies of the evolution of three curricula, looking at the divergent paths their developers followed, the issues they faced, and how they resolved these issues. Finally, we offered a list of the lessons learned by experienced practitioners of network science—curriculum developers, project organizers, teachers, and researchers including ourselves.

In Part II, we explored two problematic issues that are central to inquiry-based teaching and learning: how to promote reflective discourse and how to support good use of data. We discussed methods curriculum developers and teachers might use to tackle each of these issues.

In Part III, we step back from the particulars of network science curricula to take a broader look at the use of technology in science learning. We aim to describe the role that the Internet is poised to play in supporting inquiry-based classrooms as well as to warn educators away from directions that have proved unfruitful. We start by describing broad themes that have emerged from our work concerning educational uses of the Internet and then examine how these themes play out in a particular classroom. We end with our reflections on how technological developments in education are placing a high premium on skillful teachers who are equipped to use these new technologies to promote student learning.

## WHAT WE HAVE LEARNED: THE BROAD VIEW

Our thinking has evolved during the 4 years of research leading to this volume. We are less convinced today that the Internet will provide an easy route to improved learning; we have come to believe that people-to-people connections and especially face-to-face communication play a central role in learning. On the other hand, we have become even more impressed by the power of the technology and remain convinced that this power will ultimately be harnessed for the improvement of education. While technology evolves quickly, however, the human ability to understand, shape, and incorporate these changes evolves slowly. Access to distant resources—experts, peers, teachers, texts, images, and data—is rapidly becoming commonplace, but the understanding of how to make good use of these resources is only slowly emerging. The time required for the development, refinement, and adoption of appropriate new pedagogies may be a decade or more.

To our colleagues on this long journey—project organizers, curriculum developers, researchers, and teachers—we pass along six recommendations. Based on our research, these recommendations reflect the conclusions of the case studies in chapter 2, the lessons identified in chapter 3, the perspectives on reflective discourse developed in chapter 4, and the strategies outlined in chapter 5 for bringing students to the data. Although we ground these recommendations in our research on network science curricula, we seek to apply them toward educational uses of technology generally and toward use of the Internet in science education specifically.

## Use the Internet to broaden the context of locally grounded inquiry.

For curriculum to use the Internet effectively, it should employ the Internet as a supportive context for extending student inquiries. Students can now investigate almost any topic using resources available on the Internet. However, teachers and curriculum developers should anchor initial investigations in local phenomenon so that the concepts involved remain comprehensible and meaningful to students.

## Maintain the classroom, not the online community, as the primary learning environment.

The most effective network science curricula foster a strong sense of inquiry within a classroom rather than among distant classes. The locus of the inquiry is in the classroom with extensions into the local community; teachers are responsible for developing appropriate classroom norms and mentoring the inquiry process. The network provides resources in the forms of expertise, data, and information, all of which support and extend classroom-based inquiry.

## Provide teachers and students with multiple entry points for technology use and curriculum.

The complexities of technology use in classrooms challenge teachers. In the past, we have encouraged some teachers to learn how to use these technologies while they make significant changes in their curriculum and pedagogy. Yet many of the most effective teachers have taken 3 to 5 years to make these inter-related changes. In designing innovative curricula that make use of new technology, developers should keep this long transition in mind and create materials with multiple entry points to accommodate teachers' developing expertise with each component.

Some new curriculum initiatives have created successful models for teacher professional development to support this growth, including workshops with ongoing support, tutorials in teacher guides, online training workshops, and access to telephone and e-mail help lines. These successful models should be emulated.

The technology skills of teachers are likely the least difficult problem to solve. Teachers are starting to climb the technology curve more rapidly as computer technology becomes readily accessible, easier to use, and integrated into all aspects of their daily life.

## Help students locate educationally productive Internet resources.

One of the most common arguments for connecting schools to the Internet stresses the benefit of giving students access to a vast store of information. Too often, however, students who access information via the Internet get in over their heads, finding little of relevance or appropriate to their knowledge level. Some curriculum developers now provide teachers and students with pointers to conceptually appropriate web sites and browser frames that keep relevant information in front of students as they move from site to site.

## Use data to deepen student inquiries.

Network science has tended to focus on the problem of getting data to students, skirting the issue of how to get students analyzing data. Furthermore, curricular support when offered has consisted mostly of advice on how to make or interpret various types of statistics and displays. Curriculum developers and teachers should avoid giving recipes for data analysis and should instead emphasize the role of judgment, hypothetical thinking, and critical reasoning in examining data.

Two key suggestions emerge from our research. First, students need a reason to analyze data—a question they want answered. For this reason, it is important to involve students initially in investigations of phenomena with which they have some familiarity. Their prior knowledge and beliefs form the basis for expectations about what the data will show, setting the stage for them to be surprised by what they see and encouraged by what they find.

Second, the ease with which students can analyze data is dependent on a number of factors which teachers and curriculum developers should consider as they select investigations for students or direct students in selecting their own. In particular, students experience more difficulty analyzing data when those data are abstract in nature, use unfamiliar units, contain subtle trends, and include numerous errors that mask any trends that do exist. Surprisingly, we have found that teachers and curriculum developers typically do not analyze data before giving them to students. Correcting this common practice would go a long way in solving many of the problems that students, teachers, and developers encounter.

## Use of the Internet should reflect what we know about student learning.

Although the metaphors of *student as scientist* and *students surfing the Net* have been compelling for some, they are not anchored in what we already know about how students learn. For example, we know that teachers and curriculum developers should work to help students define one or more guiding questions for their work, and that curriculum should be driven by conceptually appropriate questions and offer a suitable degree of complexity to sustain the inquiry.

Educators must be careful not to confuse easy access to resources with learning. Student use of sophisticated or complex data sets and information can lead them into topics that are not comprehensible. The appeal of using technology needs to be tempered with careful consideration of the benefits teachers or curriculum developers expect. Technology opens many doors; educators need to be prudent in their choices about which doors to enter.

Let us turn now to look at how these themes are realized by real students and teachers working in the complex institutions called schools.

## DEBRA'S CLASS

The following two-part vignette is the story of science and math learning in a class taught by Debra, an elementary school teacher. Debra is not a fictional character but a composite of some of the teachers with whom we have had the privilege to work and in whose classrooms we have observed.

As we first meet Debra, she is already a teacher widely regarded as accomplished and skilled in inquiry-based teaching. Debra's class is functioning well, using computers in limited ways and without any online connection. We come back and look at the same classroom 3 years later to see the ways in which Debra has strengthened her teaching through the integration of technology.

### Inquiry-Based Teaching and Learning: Initial View

*Debra is a well-respected teacher at Brookside Elementary School with more than a decade of experience teaching young students. Like many other teachers, she has at one time or another taught every subject. In the last few years, she has specialized in math and science.*

*Until she attended a summer workshop on ecology 2 years ago, she like her students had little idea about the rich diversity of life present in the area immediately surrounding the school. Now alert to the possibilities, each spring Debra has her class study wildlife in the vicinity. The ecology unit is an integral part of her goal to help students appreciate the local environment, learn the interrelations of species in a given area, and master basic plant and animal taxonomy.*

*Drawing ideas from a variety of curriculum guides including Schoolyard Ecology (from GEMS) and Eco-Inquiry (from the Institute of Ecosystem Studies), Debra bases her unit on the question, "Who lives here at school with us?" She begins with the students working in teams to identify plants and animals. Science curriculum goals relating to ecology, biology, and geology are fulfilled as the students conduct extensive field investigations. The district-required math objectives regarding measurement and area coordinate with these investigations as students note sizes of specific species in field guides and practice measuring areas as they mark off their study sites.*

*The students are generally enthusiastic about this work and enjoy having the outdoor sessions as a part of their class work. Because Debra carefully structured student groups, discipline problems are rare. The students work well in their assigned roles within small groups and take responsibility for figuring out when and how to use available equipment: hand lenses, field guides, measurement tools, and research journals. Following the fieldwork, Debra and her students engage in class sessions to discuss and share what they have found. The students make regular reference to CD-ROMs and frequently choose to use ecology simulations (recommended by the school's computer coordinator) in their assigned weekly computer time slot. Although these simulations do not advance key curriculum goals, they are popular with the students, many of whom had not used computers in the earlier grades.*

*The ecology unit culminates in students creating museum-style displays that detail the life forms present in each area of the schoolyard. On presentation day, the classroom is filled with pressed leaves, photographs of animal tracks and birds seen in the area, and terraria holding pill bugs and other insects. Because each team of students has been assigned to a different part of the grounds, the sharing session highlights the diversity of habitats within the schoolyard.*

*Despite the many compliments from her principal, parents, and colleagues, Debra thinks that the presentations are too formulaic and lack the excitement that motivated the student investigations in the first place. Furthermore, she is looking for ways to extend her students' understanding of ecology well beyond what they learn from studying their local site.*

## Inquiry-Based Teaching and Learning: Three Years Later

*As Debra continues to grow as a teacher, she defines a clear goal to motivate her evolving curriculum: She seeks out ways for her students to develop a broader and deeper understanding of ecology. As part of her strategy for realizing this goal, she enlarges the set of resources available to students, including many posted on the Internet. In this endeavor, she is aided by Jill, the educational technologist who joined the school staff 2 years ago.*

*The school district's decision to replace the role of computer coordinator with that of educational technologist reflects a significant shift in the school district's priorities. Whereas the computer coordinator kept the computers running, showed faculty how to use them, and recommended software for purchase, the educational technologist is an experienced classroom teacher who works with teachers to integrate technology into their curricula. Jill has helped Debra reshape her science and math curricula to incorporate new possibilities afforded by technology. In the past, computers were used as an occasional reference source and as a recreational device. Now, most class projects make frequent use of computers. In her math curriculum, Debra has identified key skills, concepts, and tools that students require in their science investigations, including data analysis software that helps students record and organize data and represent these visually.*

*With computers in use in classrooms throughout the school, students are able to build on their skills from one year to the next. Debra can count on her fourth graders to know how to use a word processor and a web browser and reasonably expects many to solve common technology glitches as these occur. The fifth-grade teachers, in turn, have revised their curriculum to make use of their incoming* students' skills, especially their ability to work with software that organizes and represents data.

Involvement in online curricula and resources has provided the larger context Debra was hoping to find. Two years ago, Debra learned about Journey North at a regional NSTA conference. She chose to add several of the Journey North investigations to her existing unit, knowing that her students would be excited to participate with other students across the country. Indeed, their investigations of signs of spring, including when tulips first bloom and when monarch butterflies return from Mexico, have been successful. Debra appreciates the way her students can generate their own questions around each of these investigations and analyze data from the web site to pursue their questions.

Using Internet resources, students in Debra's class compare their data and observations with those from schools in other parts of the country. This year, they noticed that their tulips bloomed 2 weeks later than the same time last year. This observation puzzled the students until they noticed that no other school in their region had yet reported the blooming of their tulips. By referring to the Accu-Weather database, the students saw that March in their region was unusually cold this year, and they offered this observation to account for the delayed blooming. They then began looking at data from other regions to see if temperature data could help them predict when or where blooms would be seen first.

Monarch butterflies have also become a highlight of the local ecology unit. Debra has always found that students were attracted to them, but the school's membership in Monarch Watch has extended her ability to harness this excitement. Her fourth graders participate in a national tagging program in the fall, placing tracking tags on monarchs, some of which they grow in school and some of which they capture on the grounds. The students check the Monarch Watch web site regularly hoping to see that one of their butterflies has been recovered. Although none of theirs has yet appeared on the recovery list (fewer than 1% ever will), the students have been able to track the migration paths of tagged butterflies depicted on the national maps. These observations lead, in turn, to questions about why the monarchs follow the routes they do.

*Whereas in the past, students' work would culminate with a presentation of their observations and data, student presentations now typically include data collected by others as well. A few of the students have even developed multimedia electronic displays, which include links for downloading and adding current information. One pair of students who are following the path of an electronically tagged eagle update their page daily, allowing the class to make and test predictions about where the eagle will go next based on their understanding of the bird's migration pattern.*

*One event in particular helped Debra gauge her own success as a teacher. Based on the students' finding that tulips were blooming later this year, the students suggested that they create a local archive in which to save data collected at their school so that future students would be able to study how local habitat changes over time. Debra is pleased to see that many of her students have learned to see their locally based investigations as part of patterns.*

In this second part of the vignette, Debra's class remains substantially the same: Students are actively involved in local investigations, building understanding through firsthand experience. However, as a result of Debra's growth as a teacher, the questions that students are asking are broader in scope, deeper, and more reflective. Students' engagement in good science learning is due to Debra's skill in using the numerous resources available to the students, in helping them structure their investigations, and in mentoring the discourse in the classroom.

The addition of the technology has not driven these changes in teaching and learning but has supported them. Her students' study of ecology is still grounded in the investigation of the local ecology but is no longer confined to what they find there. Through their use of Internet resources, students are now able to compare local ecology both spatially (as they compare what lives on their school grounds with what is happening at other schools) and temporally (as they compare temperature conditions from one year to the next). In this way, the local phenomena at Debra's school are not isolated events—they occur in a pattern that makes sense geographically and seasonally. Students see the natural phenomena of spring, such as leaves budding and the lengthening of daylight hours, as part of a larger pattern of change in the environment as the season progresses.

With the Internet, Debra and her students have access to a richer set of resources than they are used to. These resources, in turn, have supported the students' use of data, including up-to-date maps and other data displays, and stimulated dialogues among the students about these data. The integration of technology into Debra's curriculum has helped students achieve the objectives of new state frameworks and national standards (e.g., that students be able to make sense of data, engage in critical writing and discussion, and employ a range of reference sources).

Looking more broadly, we see Debra as a capable professional who is building from her strength as an inquiry-based teacher to make effective use of the Internet as one of several resources to support students' work. The use of the technology did not introduce inquiry to Debra's class. Instead, her experience and expertise in the pedagogy of inquiry enabled her to employ the Internet and data analysis tools effectively. Over several years, Debra's collaboration with others, most recently with the school's educational technologist, has led to deeper inquiries and more effective integration of computers into the fabric of the classroom.

Debra is one of a growing number of teachers in her school who report that technology has created not only new ways to communicate but also new reasons to do so. Reflecting the growing sophistication of the faculty about technology and teaching, talk of surfing the Net has largely been replaced by talk of how teachers can use the Internet as a tool for supporting student investigations. Through continuing professional development, including coaching, coplanning, and coteaching with the school's educational technologist and increasingly with one another, the teachers in Debra's school are beginning to realize the promise of educational technology—to provide crucial support for deepening inquiry-based teaching and learning.

Debra's own changes as a teacher would not have been possible without the priority that the superintendent and school board placed on updating the district's curriculum and student learning goals to reflect the infusion of technology throughout the district. Debra has contributed to and benefited from this essential process of revision.

## NETWORK SCIENCE REVISITED

This vignette presents some contrasts with the founding vision of network science outlined in chapter 1. In our assessment of the founding vision, we pointed to four problematic issues that have emerged from efforts to apply it over the last decade. In light of the vignette, we consider each of these issues in turn.

### Supporting Teachers

There are many ways in which teachers develop their skills in integrating technology into the curriculum. In the vignette, two critical supports are worth emphasizing.

First, Debra adapted online curriculum resources to a content area with which she was experienced. She was already familiar with the content of ecology and with the pedagogy of inquiry, and she was able to add Internet resources as her own skills in using the Internet developed. Further, the online resources that she integrated into her classes were well suited for use by teachers and students at different skill levels. This meant that she was able to extend her and her students' use of the resources year by year as both her skills and her students' skills increased. On first getting access to the Internet, she limited herself to e-mail exchanges with experts. As she became comfortable with e-mail, she gradually added more data activities.

Second, Debra worked in a school that, like many others, recognized that teachers would need ongoing support to integrate Internet resources into their curricula. In the vignette, Debra had the support of Jill, an educational technologist. In other districts, similar support comes from library media specialists, subject-area specialists, and colleagues—in short, from others in the schools whose roles allow time for one-to-one coaching, coplanning, and coteaching. This is the key point: Debra was not learning new things in isolation, but as part of a school and district effort to reform curriculum and integrate technology use.

By contrast, we have often seen network science curricula attempt to introduce content, pedagogy, and technology simultaneously to teachers who are lone adopters in their schools with no one on site to offer assistance or encouragement. In these circumstances, even highly motivated teachers are soon overwhelmed and discouraged.

## Identifying the Community of Learners

In a networked classroom, there are multiple levels of possible collaboration. We have argued, however, that the primary focus should be on helping students in the same classroom become a community of learners, a team of inquirers who listen carefully to each other, challenge, and encourage—in short, who learn together. This type of interaction, and the kind of dialogue that characterizes it, does not spontaneously occur among students over the network. In fact, it does not spontaneously occur in the classroom either, but requires active involvement by the teacher.

Viewing classrooms such as Debra's as a community of learners stands in sharp contrast to more traditional views where the roles of teachers and students were fixed and clearly differentiated. The teacher's role in the community of practice is not to deliver information, but to help organize and structure the community in order to co-construct understanding through collaborative discourse. A community of practice builds on the strengths and experiences that each member brings to the group and the learning that is supported within the group under the guidance of a mentor.

This perspective of community of practice also departs from the *student-as-scientist* metaphor that drew from the intellectual and social roles of scientists to infer how students should approach science. Although useful historically in creating support among educators for a more active role of students as learners, the metaphor has, in practice, encouraged a level of sophistication in content that has proved inappropriate for many students.

We believe that the community-of-practice perspective will prove far more helpful in envisioning good teaching practices than the metaphor of student as scientist used in the founding vision of network science.

## Making Data Meaningful

Debra has integrated the teaching of math concepts into many parts of her curriculum, including science. With increasing fluency, her students are able to reason about data across a range of topics. Students use these skills and concepts extensively in their study of local ecology as they make counts of animals such as birds and interpret plots that highlight geographic variation and changes over time.

Data analysis is an interactive process of raising empirical questions and looking at data. Debra, reflecting her growing expertise with the subject matter, has become adept at helping students develop and apply this perspective. When some students were puzzled about the tulips blooming so late, they wondered if cold weather were to blame. In years past, the investigation would have stopped at that point, but Debra now encourages students to follow up on their hunches when possible. In this case, they explored the temperature hypothesis by accessing weather data available online. We have observed too often that network science curricula are taught in isolation from the math curriculum and that requisite quantitative skills and concepts are typically not available when needed in the science curricula. We have also observed many network science classrooms in which teachers have failed to establish and then keep in the forefront a reason for students to look at data. As a result, students are merely going through the motions of data analysis. Working with data that are only remotely connected to their own experiences, students (and sometimes their teachers) easily lose sight of the critical links among the question, the experience, and the data that make inquiry compelling and data analysis rewarding.

## Engaging Students in Productive Inquiry

Debra is an effective teacher because she can motive and support her students in asking questions and constructing answers. She knows that effective student inquiry relies on:

- students' existing knowledge base and interests—they must know something to spark the question
- her subject-area expertise—she herself must have sufficient conceptual background to understand her students' questions and support their learning effectively
- her knowledge of resources—she must know enough to steer her students toward existing data sets or help them create their own data sets, which can be checked with existing, reliable data sets

Debra is not concerned with whether the science is real, i.e., whether scientists already have answers to the questions that her students ask. Rather, she considers whether various investigations could spark students' interests and build on what students already know. Real science—advancing the frontiers of what is known—is difficult for scientists and rarely appropriate for students. Rather, the ideals of real science may inspire the work of students and teachers, but the focus should remain on topics that can spark student learning.

Debra also appreciates the freedom she has to use online resources (Journey North and Monarch Watch) as her students' needs dictate and not be constrained by timelines that tie her class schedule to that of other participating classes at remote locations. Flexible schedules are essential for successful implementation of network science curricula—a significant improvement over the more prescriptive formats that characterized many of the earlier network science curricula.

What is Debra thinking about network science? In classrooms like hers, the novelty of technology has begun to wear off; for these teachers, and especially for their students, the capabilities of new technologies are now taken for granted. After all, these technologies are increasingly a typical part of students' lives at home (Feldman, 1997). We expect that the same transformation will happen in more and more classrooms over the next few years as the proportion of teachers and students who regularly use computers and the Internet grows. Given this change and the transformations it will likely bring in the near future, the term *network science* will seem as arcane and redundant as *motor car*, with science curricula routinely incorporating experts online, discussions and conferencing among classes, and shared sets of data remotely accessed. Attention will appropriately shift away from the technology to the challenging issues of inquiry-based teaching and learning.

Debra no longer thinks about network science per se. Rather, she thinks about the rich and varied learning environment that she is able to create for her students and about how to use classroom and local resources as well as distant resources now available through technology. For Debra, technology is a useful means to bring learning resources to her students and enhance the potential of inquiry-based learning.

## FINAL REFLECTIONS

Public enthusiasm for getting schools on the Internet is currently based largely on the idea that students should have access to the vast information resources on the World Wide Web. This perception of great intellectual riches online has led to the belief that the Internet should become a central component of modern education—essential to preparing students for the demands of the 21st-century workplace and for keeping the nation competitive.

The empirical and theoretical issues we raise in this study challenge educators to look past this broad and well-intentioned rhetoric to ask how access to this information can help deepen students' understandings of math and science. Certainly, accessing information on the Web, viewing images and movies, and running simulations excite most students, at least initially. However, if students are to learn anything of significance from this information, their excitement must eventually prompt thoughtful questions and reflection—and hard work. This is the sort of teaching and learning that an able teacher and inquisitive peers can help students undertake. Although there is strong evidence that the Internet can provide resources to support good teaching and learning, there is no evidence that it can replace the role of teacher and peers. Our research and experiences indicate the opposite: The universe of information has grown larger and more complex because of the extraordinary capabilities of new technologies. As a consequence, students need more than ever the guidance of experienced and skillful teachers to learn to their full potential.

# References

American Association for the Advancement of Science. (1989). *Science for all Americans*. Washington, DC: Author.

American Association for the Advancement of Science. (1993). *Benchmarks for science literacy*. New York: Oxford University Press.

Berenfeld, B. (1993). A moment of glory in San Antonio. *Hands On!, 16*(2), 1, 19–21.

Biehler, R. (1993). Cognitive technologies for statistics education: Relating the perspective of tools for learning and of tools for doing statistics. In L. Brunelli & G. Cicchitelli (Eds.), *Proceedings of the first scientific meeting of the International Association for Statistical Education* (pp. 173–190). Perugia, Italy: Università di Perugia.

Bright, G. W., & Friel, S. N. (1998). Helping students interpret data. In S. P. Lajoie (Ed.), *Reflections on statistics: Learning, teaching, and assessment in grades K–12* (pp. 63–88). Mahwah, NJ: Lawrence Erlbaum Associates.

Broudy, H. S. (1988). *The uses of education*. New York: Routledge.

Bruce, B. C., & Rubin, A. (1993). *Electronic quills: A situated evaluation of using computers for writing in classrooms*. Hillsdale, NJ: Lawrence Erlbaum Associates.

Bruner, J. (1962). *On knowing*. Cambridge, MA: Belknap.

Bruner, J. (1971). *The relevance of education*. New York: W. W. Norton.

Burge, C. (1997, December 23). E-mail communication to Cliff Konold.

Bybee, R. W. (1987). Science education and the science-technology-society theme. *Science Education, 71*(5), 667–683.

Carpenter, T. P., & Franke, M. L. (1998). Teachers as learners. Principled practice in mathematics and science education, *NCISLA/Mathematics & Science Semiannual Newsletter, 2*(2), 1–3.

Cleveland, W. S. (1993). *Visualizing data*. Summit, N.J.: Hobart Press.

Cobb, P. (1998). *Individual and collective mathematical development: The case of statistical data analysis*. Paper presented at the annual meeting of the International Group for the Psychology of Mathematics Education, Steelenbosch, South Africa.

Cobb, P., & Bauersfeld, H. (1995). Introduction: The coordination of psychological and sociological perspectives in mathematics education. In P. Cobb & H. Bauersfeld (Eds.), *The emergence of mathematical meaning: Interaction in classroom cultures* (pp. 1–16). Hillsdale, NJ: Lawrence Erlbaum Associates.

Cobb, P., Wood, T., & Yackel, E. (1989). Young children's emotional acts while engaged in mathematical problem solving. In D. B. McLeod & V. M. Adams (Eds.), *Affect and mathematical problem solving: A new perspective* (pp. 117–148). New York: Springer-Verlag.

Collins, A. (1996). Whither technology and schools? Collected thoughts on the last and next quarter centuries. In D. C. Dwyer, C. Fisher, & K. Yocam (Eds.), *Education and technology: Reflections on computing in classrooms* (pp. 51–65). San Francisco: Jossey-Bass.

Confrey, J. (1990). A review of the research on student conceptions in mathematics, science, and programming. In C. B. Cazden (Ed.), *Review of research in education* (pp. 3–56). Washington, DC: American Education Research Association.

Coulter, B. (1997a). Journey North For Great Learning. *Connect, 11*(1), 11–12.

Coulter, B. (1997b). Tracking migratory animals: Going online for environmental education. *Green Teacher 53* (Fall), 20–21.

Data explorer [Computer software]. (1998). Pleasantville, NY: Sunburst.

Dewey, J. (1910). *How we think.* Boston: Heath.

Dewey, J. (1929). *The quest for certainty.* New York: Minton, Balch & Co.

Dewey, J. (1938). *Experience and education.* New York: Macmillan.

Donnelly, E., & Wiley, J. (1997). *Journey North: A global study of wildlife migration* (teacher's manual). Washington, DC: The Annenberg/CPB Math and Science Collection.

Driver, R., & Erickson, G. (1983). Theories-in-action: Some theoretical and empirical issues in the study of students' conceptual frameworks in science. *Studies in Science Education, 10,* 37–60.

Driver, R., Guesne, E., & Tiberghien, A. (1985). *Children's ideas in science.* England: Open University Press.

The Evergreen Project. (1996). *What's It Like Where You Live?* St. Louis, MO: Author.

Fathom Dynamic Statistics [Computer software]. (1999). Emeryville, CA: Key Curriculum Press.

Feldman, A. (1994). Connecting classrooms. *Hands On!, 17*(1), 20–21.

Feldman, A. (1997). Digital kids: There's no turning back. *Hands On!, 20*(2), 1, 16–17.

Feldman, A., Johnson, L., Lieberman, D., Allen, I., & van der Hoeven, J. (1995). *Data exchange and telecollaboration: Technology in support of new models of education.* Paper presented at INET '95 conference, Honolulu, HI. [Online], www.isoc.org/hmp/paper/159/html/paper.html.

Feldman, A., & McWilliams, H. (1995). *Planning guide for network science.* Cambridge, MA: TERC.

Feldman, A., & Nyland, H. (1994, April). *Collaborative inquiry in networked communities: Lessons from the Alice Testbed.* Paper presented at the annual meeting of the American Educational Research Association, San Francisco, CA.

Finzer, B. (1997). E-mail correspondence to C. Konold.

Fitzpatrick, C. (1997, Fall). Can young students use GIS? *ESRI ARC News,* p. 33.

Gal, I., Rothschild, K., & Wagner, D. A. (1989). *Which group is better? The development of statistical reasoning in elementary school children.* Paper presented at the meeting of the Society for Research in Child Development, Kansas City, MO.

Goodman Research Group, Inc. (1998). *An evaluation of the Testbed for Telecollaboration.* Cambridge, MA: Author.

Grant, C. M. (1998). *Data and graphing, on and off the computer: Beyond "just doing it."* Hanau Model Schools Partnership Research Report Number 1. [Online], modelschools.terc.edu/modelschools/template/publications/publications.cfm.

Hancock, C., Kaput, J. J., & Goldsmith, L. T. (1992). Authentic inquiry with data: Critical barriers to classroom implementation. *Educational Psychologist, 27*(3), 337–364.

Harasim, L., Hiltz, S. R., Teles, L., & Turoff, M. (1995). *Learning networks: A field guide to teaching and learning online.* Cambridge, MA: MIT Press.

Hawkins, D. (1965a, February). Messing about in science. *Science and Children,* 5–9.

Hawkins, D. (1965b, Summer). On living in trees. *The Colorado Quarterly,* 5–23.

Hawkins, D. (1974). I, thou, it: Mathematics teaching. In D. Hawkins, *The informed vision: Essays on learning and human nature* (pp. 48-62). New York: Agathon Press.

Healy, J. (1998). *Failure to connect: How computers affect our children's minds—for better or for worse.* New York: Simon & Schuster.

Hughes, P. (1997, December 18). Interview with Cliff Konold.

Howard, E. (1998, August 18). Personal communication with Bob Coulter.

Hunt, E. B., & Minstrell, J. (1995). *Developing self-propagating networks for instruction in science.* Project proposal submitted to the James S. McDonnell Foundation. [Online], weber.u.washington.edu/~huntlab/networks/index.html.

Hunter, B. (1993). Collaborative inquiry in networked communities. *Hands On!, 16*(2), 16–18.

Johnson, R., Brooker, C., Stutzman, J., Hultman, D., & Johnson, D. W. (1985). The effects of controversy, concurrence seeking, and individualistic learning on achievement and attitude change. *Journal of Research in Science Teaching, 22*(3), 197–205.

Julyan, C. (1988). The creation of a curriculum. *Hands On!, 11*(1), 6, 20.

Julyan, C. (1990). Lunchroom garbage: Findings from student-scientists. *Hands On!, 13*(1), 11–14.

Julyan, C. (1991). Getting connected to science. *Hands On!, 14*(1), 4–7.

Julyan, C. (1993). Mapping a journey to understanding. *Hands On!, 16*(2), 4–7.

Karlan, J. W. (1995, April 4). E-mail message to National Geographic and TERC.

Karlan, J. W., Huberman, M., & Middlebrooks, S. H. (1997). The challenges of bringing the Kids Network to the classroom. In S. A. Raizen & E. D. Britton (Eds.), *Bold ventures: Case studies of U.S. innovations in science education* (pp. 247–394). Dordecht: Kluwer Academic Publishers.

Kilpatrick, W. H. (1918). The project method. *Teachers College Record, 19,* 319–351.

Konold, C. (1995). Confessions of a coin flipper and would-be instructor. *The American Statistician, 49,* 203–209.

Konold, C. & Miller, C. DataScope [Computer software]. (1994). Santa Barbara, CA: Intellimation. Also available at: www.umass.edu/srri/serg/.

Konold, C., Pollatsek, A., Well, A., & Gagnon, A. (1997). Students analyzing data: Research of critical barriers. In J. B. Garfield & G. Burrill (Eds.), *Research on the role of technology in teaching and learning statistics: Proceedings of the 1996 IASE Round Table Conference* (pp. 151–167). Voorburg, The Netherlands: International Statistical Institute.

Koschmann, T. (1996). Paradigm shifts and instructional technology: An introduction. In T. Koschmann (Ed.), *CSCL: Theory and practice* (pp. 1–24), Hillsdale, NJ: Lawrence Erlbaum Associates.

Lajoie, S. P. (Ed.). (1998). *Reflections on statistics: Learning, teaching, and assessment in grades K–12.* Mahwah, NJ: Lawrence Erlbaum Associates.

Lave, J., & Wenger, E. (1991). *Situated learning: Legitimate peripheral participation.* Cambridge, England: Cambridge University Press.

Lehrer, R., & Romberg, T. (1996). Exploring children's data modeling. *Cognition and Instruction, 14*(1), 69–108.

Leichtweis, K. (1998, March 19). Telephone interview with Nancy London.

Lenk, C. (1989). Telecommunications in the classroom. *Hands On!, 12*(1), 1, 16–17.

Levin, J. A., Rogers, A., Waugh, M. L., & Smith, K. (1989). Observations on educational electronic networks: The importance of appropriate activities for learning. *The Computing Teacher, 16,* 17–21.

Lieberman, G. A., & Hoody, L. L. (1998). *Closing the achievement gap: Using the environment as an integrating context for learning.* San Diego: State Education and Environment Roundtable.

Linn, M. (1995, July 28). Personal communication to Alan Feldman.

Little, J. W. (1993). Teachers' professional development in a climate of educational reform. *Educational Evaluation and Policy Analysis, 15*(2), 129–151.

Logical journey of the zoombinis [Computer software]. (1996). Novato, CA: Broderbund.

McMahon, T. (1996.) *From isolation to interaction? Computer-mediated communications and teacher professional development* (unpublished doctoral dissertation, Indiana University). Indiana: Author.

Mehan, H. (1979). *Learning lessons: Social organization in the classroom.* Cambridge, MA: Harvard University Press.

Mehan, H. (1985). *Computers in classrooms: A quasi-experiment in guided change* (final report). Available from ERIC, MF01/PC12.

Mehan, H. (1989). Microcomputers in classrooms: Educational technology or social practice? *Anthropology & Education Quarterly, 20,* 4–22.

Mokros, J., & Russell, S. J. (1995). Children's concepts of average and representativeness. *Journal for Research in Mathematics Education, 26*(1), 20–39.

Moore, D. S. (1992). Teaching statistics as a respectable subject. In F. S. Gordon & S. P. Gordon (Eds.), *Statistics for the twenty-first century* (MAA Notes, #26). Washington, DC: Mathematical Association of America.

National Commission on Excellence in Education. (1983). *A nation at risk: The imperative for educational reform.* Washington, DC: Government Printing Office.

National Council of Teachers of Mathematics. (1989). *Curriculum and evaluation standards for school mathematics.* Reston, VA: Author.

National Gardening Association. (1991). *Indoor gardening: Advice from GrowLab classrooms.* Burlington, VT: Author.

National Geographic Society and TERC. (1990, 1997). *NGS Kids Network acid rain.* Washington, DC: National Geographic.

*NGS Works* [Computer software]. (1997). Washington, DC: National Geographic Society.

National Science Teachers Association. (1998). *NSTA pathways to the science standards* (middle school edition). Arlington, VA: Author.

Newman, D., Griffin, P., & Cole, M. (1989). *The construction zone: Working for cognitive change in school.* Cambridge, England: Cambridge University Press.

Oppenheimer, T. (1997, July). The computer delusion. *Atlantic Monthly, 280*(1), 45–62.

Panel on Educational Technology. (1997). *Report to the President on the use of technology to strengthen K–12 education in the United States.* Washington, DC: President's Committee of Advisors on Science and Technology.

Papert, S. (1980). *Mindstorms: Children, computers, and powerful ideas.* New York: Basic Books.

Peake, L. (1997, September 7). Interview with Brian Conroy.

Polman, J. (in press). *Guiding science expeditions: The design of a learning environment for project-based science.* New York: Teachers College Press.

Riel, M. (1985). A functional learning environment for writing. In H. Mehan (Ed.), *Computers in classrooms: A quasi-experiment in guided change* (final report). Available from ERIC, MF01/PC12.

Rosebery, A. S., & Warren, B. (Eds.). (1996). *Sense making in science (professional development resource package)*. Portsmouth, NH: Heinemann.

Rosebery, A. S., & Warren, B. (Eds.). (1998). *Boats, balloons, and classroom video.* Portsmouth, NH: Heinemann.

Roth, W.-M., & Bowen, G. M. (1994). Mathematization of experience in a grade 8 open-inquiry environment: An introduction to the representational practices of science. *Journal of Research in Science Teaching, 31,* 293–318.

Rowe, M. B. (1983). Science education: A framework for decision-makers. *Daedelus, 112*(2), 123–142.

Russell, S. J. (1990). Issues in training teachers to teach statistics in the elementary school: A world of uncertainty. In A. Hawkins (Ed.), *Training teachers to teach statistics.* Proceedings of the International Statistical Institute Round Table Conference (pp. 59–71). Voorburg, The Netherlands: International Statistical Institute.

Scardamalia, M., & Bereiter, C. (1996). Computer support for knowledge-building communities. In T. Koschmann (Ed.), *CSCL: Theory and practice* (pp. 249–268). Hillsdale, NJ: Lawrence Erlbaum Associates.

Schoenfeld, A., Minstrell, J., & van Zee, E. H. (1996). *Toward a comprehensive model of the teaching process: The detailed analysis of an established teacher's nontraditional lesson.* Paper presented at the annual meeting of the American Educational Research Association, New York, NY.

Shaughnessy, J. M. (1992). Research in probability and statistics: Reflections and directions. In D. Grouws (Ed.), *Handbook of research on the teaching and learning of mathematics* (pp. 465–494). New York: Macmillan.

SimCity [Computer software]. (1994). Walnut Creek, CA: Maxis.

Simon, M. A. (1995). Reconstructing mathematics pedagogy from a constructivist perspective. *Journal of Research in Mathematics Education, 26*(2), 114–145.

Smith, R. C., & Taylor, E. F. (1995). Teaching physics on line. *American Journal of Physics, 63*(12), 1090–1096.

Sneider, C., & Golden, R. (1999). *Global systems science: Changing climate.* Berkeley, CA: Lawrence Hall of Science, University of California. (Available from NASA Teacher Resource Centers and NASA CORE.)

Soloway, E., & Wallace, R. (1997). Does the Internet support student inquiry? Don't ask. *Communications of the ACM, 40*(5), 11–16.

Statistics workshop [Computer software]. (1992). Pleasantville, NY: Sunburst.

Stubbes, M. (1983). *Discourse analysis: The sociological analysis of natural language.* Chicago: University of Chicago Press.

Tabletop [Computer software]. (1995). Novato, CA: Broderbund.

TERC. (1986). *KIDNET.* A proposal submitted to the National Science Foundation. Cambridge, MA: Author.

TERC. (1989). *A pilot network for global education.* A proposal submitted to the National Science Foundation. Cambridge, MA: Author.

TERC. (1991). *The global lab curriculum.* A proposal submitted to the National Science Foundation. Cambridge, MA: Author.

TERC. (1996). *Investigations in number, data, and space.* Palo Alto, CA: Dale Seymour Publications.

TERC. (1997). *Global lab curriculum: An integrated science course* (prepublication version). Cambridge, MA: Author.

TERC. (1999). *Acid rain* (pre-publication version for National Geographic Kids Network). Cambridge, MA: Author.

Testbed for Telecollaboration. (Eds.). (1997). *Responses from conference participants.* [Online], teaparty.terc.edu/conference/materials/response.html.

Tinker, R. F. (1987a). Network science arrives. *Hands On!, 10*(1), 1, 10–11.

Tinker, R. F. (1987b). Real science education. *Hands On!, 10*(1), 2.

Tinker, R. F. (1988). The gap between science and education. *Hands On!, 11*(1), 2, 22.

Tinker, R. F. (1989). Network science. *Hands On!, 12*(1), 6, 19.

Tinker, R. F. (1990). Modeling and real science: Helping students build and test their own theories. *Hands On!, 13*(1), 15, 20–21.

Tinker, R. F. (1993a). Educational networking: Images from the frontier. *Hands On!, 16*(1), 6–8, 19.

Tinker, R. F. (1993b). Curriculum development and the scientific method. *Hands On!, 16*(2), 2.

Tukey, J. W. (1977). *Exploratory data analysis.* Reading, MA: Addison-Wesley.

van Zee, E. H., & Minstrell. J. (1997a). Reflective discourse: Developing shared understandings in a physics classroom. *International Journal of Science Education, 19*(2), 209–228.

van Zee, E. H., & Minstrell. J. (1997b). Using questions to guide student thinking. *The Journal of the Learning Sciences, 6*(2), 227–269.

Varelas, M. (1996). Between theory and data in a seventh-grade science class. *Journal of Research in Science Teaching, 33*(3), 229–263.

Vesel, J. (1998, January 13). Interview with Nancy London and Alan Feldman.

Vincent, A. (1999, September 7). Interview with Alan Feldman.

von Glasersfeld, E. (1984). An introduction to radical constructivism. In P. Watzlawick (Ed.), *The invented reality* (pp. 17–40). New York: Norton.

Walters, J. M. (1996). *Final report on the EnergyNet project* (unpublished report). Cambridge, MA: TERC.

Wasser, J. D., & Bresler, L. (1996). Working in the interpretive zone: Conceptualizing collaboration in qualitative research teams. *Educational Researcher, 25*(5), 5–15.

Watson, J. M., & Moritz, J. B. (1998). *The beginning of statistical inference: Comparing two data sets* (unpublished manuscript). Hobart, Tasmania: Author.

Wenglinsky, H. (1998). *Does it compute? The relationship between educational technology and student achievement in mathematics.* Princeton, NJ: Educational Testing Services.

Whitehead, A. N. (1929). *The aims of education.* New York: The Free Press.

Williams, J. (1995). *USA Today weather almanac.* New York: Vintage Books.

Yager, R. E. (1984). Toward new meaning for school science. *Educational Leadership, 41*(4), 12–18.

Young, V., Haertel, G., Ringstaff, C., & Means, B. (1998, October). *Evaluating global lab curriculum: Impacts and issues of implementing a project-based science curriculum* (review draft). Menlo Park, CA: SRI International.

# Appendix A:
# Project Descriptions

From 1992 to 1997, research staff from both Testbed projects worked closely with network science projects. Staff visited classrooms and interviewed teachers and students and conferred frequently with project staff and curriculum writers. These five projects listed next were central to our research.

### CLASSROOM BIRDWATCH (formerly Classroom FeederWatch)

Developed by Cornell Lab of Ornithology (the Lab), Classroom BirdWatch is an interdisciplinary data-collection project for students in Grades 5 to 8. Pilot and field-test versions of the project were developed in conjunction with TERC. Students count the kinds and numbers of birds that visit feeders in their schoolyard from mid-November to the end of February and report this information via the Internet (web-based forms) to the Lab. The data collected from this project each year helps ornithologists track changes in the abundance and distribution of bird species that use feeders in winter. Thus, students contribute authentic data to a central database used by professional ornithologists; in the process, they learn how science and scientists work. Curriculum materials are currently available from the Cornell Lab. Classroom BirdWatch was funded by the National Science Foundation. For more information: birdsource.cornell.edu/cfw/.

## ENERGYNET

In EnergyNet, students from Grades 6 to 12 in Illinois examine issues of energy use in their schools and create policy recommendations for their school districts. Students conduct energy audits of their schools, share their data through a web-based data submittal/retrieval system, and analyze their findings to determine potential ways to make their school buildings more energy-efficient. EnergyNet students have the opportunity to influence local energy policy by making presentations to their local school boards. Students develop problem-solving and team-building skills through these activities. The project also aims to familiarize students with new Internet and computer technologies. Curriculum materials are available from the project organizer. EnergyNet was funded through a combination of corporate and Illinois state sources. For more information: www.energynet.org.

## GLOBAL LAB: An Integrated Science Course

*Global Lab: An Integrated Science Course* is an interdisciplinary environmental science curriculum for Grades 8 to 10 through which students engage in real-world investigations. Although they conduct these investigations at a local level, students broaden their understanding of their environment by having them compare their research findings to those of students all over the world. Students telecommunicate with others in the Global Lab community by sharing data via web-based forms and through GL Voices—an online bulletin board. Global Lab emphasizes students doing real science activities—using authentic scientific instrumentation and engaging in open-ended investigations. As the year progresses, students take on increasingly greater responsibility for designing and analyzing the results of their investigations. The curriculum culminates with groups of students conducting their own research projects. The development of Global Lab was funded by the National Science Foundation. For more information: globallab.terc.edu.

# NATIONAL GEOGRAPHIC KIDS NETWORK

NGS Kids Network, a collaboration between the National Geographic Society (NGS) and TERC, is the original network science project. First published in the late 1980s for elementary grades and revised and extended in 1997 to include middle grades, Kids Network is a series of collaborative, interdisciplinary science units in which students explore real-world topics by conducting experiments, analyzing data, and sharing results worldwide. Each unit engages students in hands-on activities; the data from these activities are used to develop science content and process. Classes share letters and data via the Internet with classes in other schools and analyze the composite data. Through these activities, students deepen their understandings of ideas developed at the local level. *NGS Works*, a software tool for data analysis and telecommunications designed for the project, supports representation of data on graphs and maps. The development of NGS Kids Network was funded by the National Science Foundation and NGS. For more information: www.ngs.com.

## JOURNEY NORTH

*Journey North did not receive direct services from the Testbed; however, we were in close communication with the project staff, especially in the last year of research.*

Journey North is a K–12 project in which students observe, record, and exchange information about environmental changes that occur in response to seasonal change. Students witness these seasonal changes in their own communities and learn about changes across the nation by comparing their data with the data submitted by other schools. For example, Journey North students plant a tulip garden, observe when the tulips first emerged and bloomed, and then submit this information to the Journey North web site. Using this information, students create maps that show the pattern of tulip blooming across the country or access online maps created by the Journey North staff that represent the data. Another way that Journey North students gauge seasonal change is by following the migration of wild animals whose locations are reported by radio tags. Students use the reported geographical coordinates to map the animals' movements. As students carry out these activities, they learn about the interrelationship of natural systems and how these systems correspond to seasonal increases in energy from the sun. Resource binders are available for teachers, and all materials are posted at the project's web site. Journey North is funded by the Annenberg/CPB Math and Science Project. For more information: www.learner.org/jnorth/.

# Appendix B:
# Network Science Conference

From November 6 to November 7, 1997, a group of 33 curriculum developers, project organizers, teachers, researchers, and funders of network science projects gathered at TERC to discuss the state of the art and the future directions of network science and to share their experiences across a diverse set of network science projects. Key points from the conference have informed the lessons learned as described in chapter 3.

| Name | Project | Organization |
|------|---------|--------------|
| Alan Feldman, Conference cochair | Testbed for Telecollaboration | TERC |
| Cliff Konold, Conference cochair | Testbed for Telecollaboration | TERC |
| Rick Bonney | Classroom BirdWatch | Cornell Lab of Ornithology |
| Lisa Christie | Researcher | Goodman Research Group (Cambridge, MA) |
| Brian Conroy | Testbed for Telecollaboration | TERC |

| Name | Project | Organization |
|------|---------|--------------|
| Bob Coulter | Teacher involved in Journey North, Leveraging Learning, Highway to the Tropics, Math Forum, Online Mentor, Blue Ice: Antarctica | Forsyth School (St. Louis, MO) |
| Tim Donahue | Project organizer | Global Rivers Environmental Education Network (GREEN) |
| Teon Edwards | Global Lab | TERC |
| Vicki Golburgh | Teacher involved in Global Lab | Horace Mann Middle School (Franklin, MA) |
| Topher Hagemeier | Leveraging Learning | TERC |
| Joel Halvorson | Journey North | Science Museum of Minnesota |
| Jay Holmes | International Education and Resource Network (I*EARN) | American Museum of Natural History, Education Department |
| Candace Julyan | Community Science Connection | Arnold Arboretum (Boston, MA) |
| James Karlan | Environmental Studies Department | Antioch New England Graduate School |
| Abbey Koplovitz | Schoolyard Ornithology Resource Project (SORP) | TERC |
| Meredith Kusch | Classroom BirdWatch | Cornell Lab of Ornithology |
| Roslyn Leibensperger | Classroom BirdWatch | Cornell Lab of Ornithology |
| Karen Leichtweis | Journey North | Annenberg/CPB Math and Science Project |

| Name | Project | Organization |
|------|---------|--------------|
| Nancy London | Testbed for Telecollaboration | TERC |
| Deborah Muscella | LabNet | TERC |
| Caroline Nobel | Project organizer | American Museum of Natural History, Education Department |
| Ray Rose | Virtual High School, International Netcourse Teacher Enhancement Coalition (INTEC) | The Concord Consortium |
| Perry Samson | The Weather Underground Virtual Classroom | University of Michigan |
| Tham Yoke-Chun | ScienceALIVE | Singapore Ministry of Education, Educational Technology Division |
| Than Jor Lan | ScienceALIVE | Singapore Ministry of Education, Educational Technology Division |
| Carol Timms | EnergyNet | Coalition 2000 (Illinois) |
| Deborah Trumbull | Classroom BirdWatch | Cornell Lab of Ornithology |
| Judy Vesel | Leveraging Learning, Classroom BirdWatch, Schoolyard Ornithology Resource Project (SORP) | TERC |
| Joe Walters | Global Lab | TERC |
| Susan Wheelwright | Teacher involved in Journey North | Fayerweather Street School (Cambridge, MA) |

# Appendix C:
# Goodman Research Group
# Evaluation Report

Goodman Research Group, Inc. (GRG) was contracted by TERC to conduct an external evaluation of the Testbed for Telecollaboration during the project's final year of field-based operation (1996–1997). For this evaluation, GRG examined five different network science projects to assess the Testbed's success at supporting data-rich telecollaborative projects. In conducting this five-project meta-analysis, GRG compared three projects that were supported directly by the Testbed (Classroom BirdWatch, Global Lab and EnergyNet) with two other network science projects (Journey North and EnviroNet). GRG also investigated the Testbed's effectiveness in transferring the data-sharing infrastructure that supported these projects. The final report was completed in the spring of 1998 and is available on request from TERC. The executive summary follows.

## EXECUTIVE SUMMARY

### Introduction

Testbed for Telecollaboration, a research project funded by the National Science Foundation, seeks to involve science classrooms around the country working together to design experiments, gather and share their data, and analyze the results. Students and teachers communicate using World Wide Web browsers. The target audience is teachers of Grades 4 to 12 who teach project-based, inquiry-oriented science and mathematics or who are interested in doing so. The Testbed is part of TERC in Cambridge, Massachusetts, and funding began September 1994. It is currently in its final year of funding.

The overarching goal of the Testbed for Telecollaboration project, hereafter referred to as the Testbed, has been to establish network science as an effective educational technology ready for widespread implementation. *Network science* is the term used to describe inquiry-based learning and teaching among classrooms at geographically distant sites working collaboratively to explore a shared problem. Reflecting this goal, the Testbed has had four objectives:

- to develop the organizational infrastructure to support network science;
- to develop the technology infrastructure to support network science;
- to research and document new models of telecollaboration and examine their effectiveness; and
- to disseminate implementation guides and research results.

## External Evaluation

TERC contracted Goodman Research Group, Inc. of Cambridge, Massachusetts, in late November 1996 to serve as the external evaluator during the final year of the Testbed for Telecollaboration project. GRG sought to conduct a meta-evaluation of five telecollaborative projects. The three Testbed projects participating in the evaluation were Classroom BirdWatch, EnergyNet, and Global Lab curricula. The two participating non-Testbed projects were EnviroNet and Journey North. Key objectives of the evaluation of the Testbed have been to examine:

1. the effectiveness of the support the Testbed provided for conducting data-rich investigations;
2. the willingness of the individual curriculum projects or other organizations to take over where the Testbed left off; and
3. the suitability of the projects for wider implementation.

The evaluation used multiple methods for obtaining data about the projects:

- surveys/interviews with teachers participating in these projects
- site visits to selected teachers and their students during project classes
- interviews with project directors and other staff
- data from the Testbed-sponsored conference at TERC of selected telecollaborative projects
- secondary data from individual project evaluators/research staff

## RESULTS

### Perspectives of Project Teachers

We have survey data from 58 teachers: 17 who used Classroom BirdWatch (CBW), 9 EnergyNet (EN), 10 Global Lab (GL), 12 EnviroNet (EV), and 10 Journey North (JN).

Teachers' primary motivation for participation was either to meet the needs of the students or enhance their own professional growth. Teachers wanted to participate to provide authentic learning for their students.

Teachers wanted students to gain a better grasp of science concepts (55%), gain a world view (43%), or experience authentic science (32%).

Almost three quarters (72%) of the respondents cited barriers to participation that they had either overcome or with which they were consistently struggling. The barriers included computer access, data collection, and administrative support.

Many teachers indicated that they participated in these projects to provide students an opportunity to work with data. There was little variation across projects in the data sources (from project staff, other classes, or their own data) that the teachers used.

Nearly three quarters of the teachers said they checked data for accuracy, whereas 27% of respondents indicated they did not check.

Almost all (98%) received some form of support during their participation. A majority (78%) indicated they felt supported in their efforts to use the projects.

A majority of respondents (80%) indicated that the project had affected the way they teach by providing actual curriculum materials or by reinforcing what they were already doing.

Nearly half of the teachers mentioned [that] students gained data analysis skills, whereas only a quarter mentioned understanding the curriculum's content as a student outcome.

Three quarters said the projects could not be done without the Internet component. Even those who said the project could be done without the Internet also stated the projects would not have been as effective (or even the same project) without the Internet.

## Testbed Versus Non-Testbed Projects

One of the objectives of this evaluation was to compare experiences of teachers in Testbed (CFW, EN, GL) and non-Testbed (EV, JN) projects. On many points, both groups were quite similar in their responses:

They were equally positive about the project and about high student interest.

About a third of teachers from both the Testbed and non-Testbed projects indicated the students had a lot of input.

Virtually all teachers from both non-Testbed and Testbed projects received some project support.

On other issues, the Testbed and non-Testbed teachers differed:

Half of the non-Testbed teachers cited professional growth as their reason for participating in the project, but no Testbed respondent mentioned this.

Non-Testbed teachers were somewhat more likely to say the project provided a global perspective.

Non-Testbed teachers used data from project staff and data posted by other classrooms more often than did Testbed teachers.

In contrast, Testbed teachers were more likely than non-Testbed teachers to use online and print support and to be satisfied with the support they received.

## Perspectives of Project Staff Members

To complement the evaluation data we collected from teachers, GRG twice interviewed by phone at least one staff member from each of the five projects. The key purpose of these interviews was to gather information about the behind the scenes project organization, network server issues, and some other technical aspects about which teachers would not necessarily be informed.

Most staff stated there were many goals associated with their own project: teaching the science content, teaching research methods, making science real, producing changes in students, bringing the world to the classroom, and teaching students about technology.

The staff stated that, although the project could be done without the Internet, the Internet greatly enhanced what students were able to do. Staff members viewed technology as a tool for enhancing the substance of their projects.

Staff believed the projects had effectively used the Internet and that the Internet broadened the students' perspectives about the world outside the classroom. They felt their projects provided excellent science content and materials.

Two areas for improvement that staff mentioned most often were the importance of developing projects that are easy to implement and the need to help teachers meet their curriculum requirements.

Staff agreed that data were important for science learning and were integral to the projects. They stated that quantitative data collection should be used only when it helps teachers do something they would not otherwise be able to do.

Professional development support was an essential element of all the projects. Online resources were seen as an important means for teachers from many parts of the country to share lessons and ideas about the projects.

Project staff stated they need to focus on funding, widespread implementation, and professional development in the future.

## CONCLUSIONS

### Network science can be viewed as a developmental process.

Network science, as defined by TERC, describes "inquiry-based learning and teaching among classrooms at geographically distant sites working collaboratively to explore a shared problem." According to our teacher and staff interviews, the missing component was that teachers were not "working collaboratively to explore a shared problem." Although the teachers were actively involved in the curriculum and Internet aspects of the project, they were not making use of each other's data. Many of them indicated they already used hands-on activities, but have trouble with data analysis on their own, let alone sharing data using the Internet.

### Inquiry-based science projects should emphasize data analysis.

Data analysis fits well with inquiry learning. We speculate that teachers' successful use of data is a developmental process. first, teachers need to practice gathering and posting their own data and become comfortable with this process. Then they need to learn how to look at larger data sets. Only when an individual classroom's data reside in a larger pool of data can one draw conclusions about the validity and reliability of classroom data and analysis. If projects wish to emphasize the global nature of data, they will need to make looking at the larger data sets an integral part of the work of the teachers and students.

### The Internet is a value-added component.

[Project staff cited use of] the Internet as one of the most successful aspects of the projects. They believed that the use of the Internet enhanced the projects tremendously. Teachers from all five projects agreed that there was great power in the Internet connection, but that it also presented frustrations. The most frustrating aspect for staff was that the teachers were rarely in situa tions (due to lack of equipment or knowledge of the required technology) in which they were able to take full advantage of the technology-based [features] of the projects. Computer access in the classroom and reliable Internet access were far less optimal than project staff had hoped.

### Required curricula and school structures create challenges for network science projects.

Teachers stated that they will adopt a supplementary curriculum if it [accommodates] at least some aspect of their required curriculum. Teachers will not use Internet projects for the sake of using the Internet. The traditional school culture presented another challenge for developers of these projects. For many teachers, the collaboration required by these projects was difficult [because of] time constraints and the fact that collaboration has not been part of public school culture.

### Initial training and ongoing support are essential.

Training and support are crucial, albeit underfunded, aspects of inquiry-based projects. Teachers need experience with learning in inquiry-based environments as well as permission to experiment and take risks in an environment that is respectful and supportive. Supports that are necessary for teachers to use technology effectively include equipment access; on-site and job-embedded technical and pedagogical assistance; time for learning, collaborating, and reflecting; policies to sustain the long haul of change; and active support from principals and administrators.

### As the projects take on the technical roles the Testbed played, some support roles still need to be filled.

Some of the projects have already assumed many of the technical support roles the Testbed staff played during the Testbed for Telecollaboration project. As this transition is completed, the projects still need some types of assistance. It may be appropriate for TERC or another outside forum to help projects make the best use of data, through tutorials and data analysis tools.

## These projects appear suitable for wider implementation.

It is clear from both teacher and staff interviews that teachers enjoyed their involvement with these projects; [teachers] reported benefiting professionally, and they also felt their students benefited from the projects. Beyond this, the projects served a need for teachers to gain experience with Internet resources that play a rapidly expanding role in schools. Given these benefits, it appears that these projects are suitable for expansion. In fact, the projects are already becoming more widely implemented, and project staff are making future plans accordingly.

## Greater dissemination is vital for expansion to occur.

One of the issues in a project such as the Testbed is how to spread the word about what occurred. Some of the partnering projects have begun to speak with the larger community of science educators. Projects should continue to expand these efforts with teachers, administrators, and policymakers.

## Network science is ready for reconceptualization.

The results of our surveys with teachers and project staff, as well as lengthy discussions during the Testbed Conference, point to the readiness of the network science model for reconceptualization. Greater emphasis on classroom-focused inquiry is key to teachers making better use of cross-classroom collaborations. The better their foundation in inquiry in their own classroom, the better positioned teachers will be to take the next step of collaborating with other classrooms.

More attention needs to be placed on grounding the curriculum in local experiences, providing professional development about inquiry-based teaching and learning, helping teachers become more comfortable with using the Internet, introducing teachers to data analysis, and modeling collaborative relationships. Furthermore, projects need to take into account the existing school structure and curricula. However, the projects provided an authentic science experience, and the projects' use of the Internet contributed to the authenticity and provided instantaneous access to global information. If the projects can build on the teachers' enthusiasm and attend to the aforementioned issues, we believe that the vision of network science—using collaborations among classrooms to strengthen inquiry-based teaching and learning—is likely to be achieved.

# Endnotes

1. See, for example, Berenfeld (1993), Feldman (1994), Hunter (1993), Julyan (1988, 1990, 1991, 1993), Lenk (1989), Tinker (1987a, 1987b, 1988, 1989, 1990, 1993a, 1993b).

2. Among the most prominent of these curricula were *Elementary Science Study* (Walcott, Hawkins, and Naiman), *Science: A Process Approach* (American Association for the Advancement of Science Commission on Science Education—Mayor and Livermore), and *Science Curriculum Improvement Study—SCIS* and *SCIIS*—(Karplus) for elementary grades; *Intermediate Science Curriculum Study* (Berkman, Redfield, and Dawson), *ERC—Life Science Investigations—Man and Environment* (Day and Harvey), *Foundational Approach in Science Teaching* (Pottenger) for middle school; and *Physical Science Study Committee—High School Physics* (Zacharias), *Chemical Bond Approach* (Strong), *Biological Sciences Curriculum Study—High School Biology* (Mayer), *Chemical Education Materials Study* (Pimental, Ridgway), and *Introductory Physical Science* (Haber-Schaim) for high school.

3. These issues may be understood better when current network science projects have completed their own evaluations, but most of the existing studies have not been made available publicly.

4. The most important sources of data for the section on NGS Kids Network include an interview with Judy Vesel, TERC's project director and curriculum director for Kids Network, on January 13, 1998; an interview with Sharon Cowley, NGS Kids Network director, on August 17, 1999; an interview with Al Vincent, president of Kendall-Hunt, on September 7, 1999; Jimmy Karlan's e-mail to NGS and TERC of April 4, 1995 detailing his proposal for major revisions of Kids Network curriculum units; Karlan, Huberman, and Middlebrooks' research study (1997); many informal conversations with Vesel and other project staff; the experience of co-author Bob Coulter as a field-test teacher and consultant for the web-based units; NGS Kids Network curriculum materials, print and online; and project proposals.

5. This vignette and the two that followed are accounts of real teachers. The names have been changed to afford anonymity.

6. The most important sources of data for the case study of Global Lab include a formal, taped interview with former project director Leigh Peake on September 7, 1997; many informal conversations with Peake and other project staff; conversations with Robin Brown, TERC's development coordinator; observations in many Global Lab classrooms and conversations with Global Lab teachers; Global Lab curriculum materials, print and online; and project proposals.

7. In 1997, the Testbed for Telecollaboration project staff anticipated Global Lab's need for a streamlined system of authoring, publishing, and community communication. The Testbed had previously developed CLEO (Collaborative Learning Environments Online), a web-based tool that facilitated classroom research by allowing students to author and publish their own investigations. The Testbed worked with Global Lab project developers to reconfigure CLEO as GLOW, an online site for exchanging data.

8. The most important sources for data for the case study of Journey North include interviews with Elizabeth Howard on March 18, 1998, and Karen Leichtweis on March 19, 1998 (taped); contributions to the Network Science Conference by Joel Halvorson; the experience of coauthor Bob Coulter as a Journey North teacher and consultant; and the Journey North web site and teacher materials.

9.  Access to messages from Global Lab teachers was provided courtesy of the Global Lab project at TERC.

10. Access to questionnaires from Classroom BirdWatch teachers was provided courtesy of Cornell Laboratory of Ornithology.

11. Wait times of 3 to 4 seconds may not seem like much, but Rowe (1983) suggested that increasing the time from 1 second to 3 seconds has a large effect on the length and types of responses students give.

12. Based on her research, Rowe (1983) recommended that even the more neutral verbal rewards such as fine and okay be used sparingly because higher rates of such rewards tend to be associated with lower quality explanations.

13. A synopsis of this research, broken down into various process and content areas, is included in chapter 15 of AAAS's (1993) *Benchmarks for Science Literacy*.

14. There are, in fact, several varieties of sociocultural perspectives on learning which we do not distinguish here. Cobb and Bauersfeld (1995) presented a concise overview of these as well as their interactionist view in which they preserve what they see as the merits of constructivist and sociocultural perspectives, depending on the problem under consideration.

15. For evidence of the pedagogical advantages of the use of controversy, see Johnson, Brooker, Stutzman, Hultman, and Johnson (1985). Fifth-grade students working in groups that debated different points of view about whether wolves should be a protected species learned more and had better attitudes about the experience than those who worked in groups with the goal of reaching a consensus on the same issue.

16. Preliminary research suggests that connecting learners who are otherwise isolated—and therefore do not have good face-to-face alternatives—may be an excellent use of online discussions.

17. Additional discussion of this issue can be found in chapter 3. See "Lesson 6: Online staff development cannot replace face-to-face communication."

18. Finzer is educational technology director at Key Curriculum Press and heads the development of the data analysis program *Fathom Dynamic Statistics* (1999) and accompanying curriculum materials for Grades 9 to 14 (see www.key-press.com/fathom).

19. We have inserted some of the plots they examined during their analysis.

20. This is an expansion of accounts found in Coulter (1997a and 1997b).

21. Coulter's background includes a doctoral degree in curriculum and teaching with a focus on integrating technology into elementary science programs and familiarity with methods of statistical analysis. Furthermore, he knew these students well, having had them in a class the previous year.

22. See Polman's (1997) dissertation for a long-term study of a high school teacher's struggle with learning how to design and manage students' projects effectively.

23. We do not mean to single out these projects. We could draw similar experiences from nearly every network science project.

24. We chose not to include a discussion of how software may help or hinder this problem. Network science classrooms that do use software for analyzing data typically use spreadsheets, and few teachers seem to be aware of how spreadsheets differ from data analysis software (Biehler, 1993). Although spreadsheets can be used to generate summary statistics and high-quality graphics, they are ill equipped for the kind of visual investigation of statistical distributions that is the hallmark of exploratory data analysis (cf. Cleveland, 1993). There are a now a number of data analysis tools designed specifically for student use. However, even with the best of these—*Data Explorer* (Sunburst, 1998), *DataScope* (Intellimation, 1994), *Fathom Dynamic Statistics* (Key Curriculum Press, 1999), *NGS Works* (National Geographic Society, 1997), *Statistics Workshop* (Sunburst, 1992), *Tabletop* (Broderbund, 1995)— students too frequently use them to search, often in trial-and-error fashion, for the right display plot (Grant, 1998) rather than explore the data.

25. For readers not familiar with these representations, the lines on either end are sometimes referred to as whiskers and the rectangle in the middle as the box. The plot partitions the data into quartiles. The left whisker extends from the smallest value to the 25th percentile. Thus, in the upper box plot for the cities along the 47th parallel, the left whisker indicates that the lowest value is about 2 and the 25th percentile is at 7 inches. The right whisker of the upper plot incorporates the upper 25% of the data, ending with the highest value of 27. The box extends from the 25th to the 75th percentiles, enclosing 50% of the data. The location of the median is indicated by the line within the box, which in the case of the upper plot is 11.

26. The example of snowfall in this chapter illustrates the conceptual difficulty of working with aggregate values. The January snowfall data are, in fact, 30-year averages for the years 1965 to 1994. This information changes how one views the data. Thinking the data were from one January, an expert might have wondered whether this had been a typical January. On learning that these are average values, an expert would take the apparent differences more seriously. However, many young students would be baffled by average snowfall. Should they still picture 6 inches of snow piled up over Reno? The risk would be that, being unsure about what averages values are, students would treat them as numbers only, stripped of their meaning.

27. Although these were the basic representations students used, the program also allowed students to form various groupings of data points. Using these capabilities, the students could, and did, partition data displayed as a stack plot into representations that were functionally equivalent to histograms and box plots.

# Author Index

# Subject Index

Classroom learning
community-of-practice perspective in, 142
interactive learning environments, 13–14, 15t
notions of audience in, 77
as the primary learning environment, 17–18
using the Internet to support, 63–64, 132–135, 137–140
See also Cross-classroom collaborations; Inquiry-based education; Reflective discourse

Classroom norms
defined, 81
online discussions and, 89
reflective discourse and, 91–92

CLEO. See Collaborative Learning Environments Online

Cognitively Guided Instruction (CGI), 96

Collaborative Learning Environments Online (CLEO), 172 (n7)

Community-of-practice paradigm, 142

Community Science Connection, 5

Computer-assisted instruction, 13–14

Computer Chronicles News Network, 4, 14

Computers, 3. See also Educational technology; Internet

Computer-Supported Collaborative Learning (CSCL), 14

Computer Supported Intentional Learning Environments (CSILE), 93

Construction zone concept, 90

Constructivism, on reflective discourse, 87–89

Content knowledge
in Global Lab Curriculum, 43–44
in staff development, 67–68

Cornell Lab of Ornithology, 68, 153

Cross-classroom collaborations
assessment of learning in, 17–18
in Classroom BirdWatch, 94
data sharing in, 8–9, 46
founding visions of, 4–8, 76–77

in Global Lab, 46–48
reality of, 77–79, 97
supporting with the Internet, 75–76
time delays and, 93
See also Online discussions

CSCL. See Computer-Supported Collaborative Learning

CSILE. See Computer Supported Intentional Learning Environments

**D**

Data
conceptual nature of, 118
minimizing errors in, 115–116
National Geographic Kids Network and, 37–38
pursuing salient trends in, 116–117
sharing and exchanging, 8–9, 46

Data plots
box plots, 122, 123
cascade of inscriptions concept, 118–119, 126
case-value bar graphs, 119, 120f, 122
guidelines for selecting, 123–126
histograms, 120, 121f, 122, 123
stack plots, 119–120, 121f, 123

Data use and analysis
assessment of, 18
fourth grade case study, 107–111
in Global Lab, 45–46
guidelines for task selection, 123–126
improving early instruction in, 100
improving student performance in, 100–101, 127
asking empirical questions, 111
basing questions on data, 112
familiarity with the conceptual nature of data, 118
familiarity with the data context, 117–118
minimizing data errors, 115–116
narrowing questions, 112
predicting what data will show, 112–114

## K

KIDNET, 4. *See also* National Geographic Kids Network

Kids as Global Scientists, xviii

## L

Lawrence Hall of Science, 97

Learning, inquiry-based. *See* Inquiry-based education

Legitimate peripheral participation concept, 90

Line plots. *See* Stack plots

Local inquiry
in curricula supporting student inquiry, 61–63
using the Internet to support, 132
*See also* Classroom learning; Student inquiry

*Logical Journey of the Zoombinis* (software), 14

*Logo-as-Latin* paradigm, 13–14

*Logo* language, 13–14

## M

Mainframe computers, 3

Mathematics Learning Forum, 70

Mentored reflective discourse
comparing to other types of classroom discussion, 85–86
example of, 81–85
overview of, 80–81
"reflective tosses," 85, 86
role of teachers in, 80–81, 82–85, 86, 88, 90–91

Mercer Island High School, 82

Migration studies. *See* Journey North

## N

NASA Teacher Resource Centers, 97

National Commission on Excellence in Education, 12–13

National Geographic Kids Network, xv
Acid Rain Unit, 7, 8, 30, 31
assessment of project choice in, 20
case example, 27
centralized scheduling and, 19
data exchange in, 8–9
development of, 4, 5
enrollment figures, 30
goals of, 11
NGS Works software, xvi, 32, 34, 155
original curriculum, 31–32
evaluation of, 32–33
project description, 28t, 30–31, 39–40, 155
project evolution
aligning with national standards, 36
current challenges, 38–39
designing new models of web use, 36–37
expanding data use by students, 37–38
integrating Internet technology, 33–34
restructuring curriculum units, 35–36
supporting classroom discussion, 37
project topics, 7, 27, 30, 39–40
publishing history, 25–26, 30–31
Science-Technology-Society approach in, 30
student-as-scientist concept in, 9–10, 40
teacher support in, 37, 68
Testbed for Telecollaboration and, xviii
web-based units, 31, 33–34, 36–37
robust technical design of, 65–66

National Geographic Society, 30, 155

National Geography Standards, 36

National Science Foundation (NSF), 4, 30, 41, 153, 154, 155

National Science Education Standards, 36

National Science Teachers Association, 20–21